ADVANCE PRAISE FOR

THE SCIENCE I KNOW: CULTURALLY RELEVANT SCIENCE LESSONS FROM SECONDARY CLASSROOMS

"Dr. Suzanna Roman-Oliver has nailed it with this book. Not only is she able to provide invaluable insights with her experiences as a K-12 teacher and a clinical assistant professor, but she does what many educators have struggled to do. Dr. Roman-Oliver aligned all of the resources in her book to NGSS standards. Educators will have access to high-quality 3D lessons that will prove to be highly engaging and interactive to each learner. If we expect our educators to teach science and engineering practices, crosscutting concepts, and disciplinary core ideas with fidelity, provide them with an opportunity to explore this great resource."

Latasha Lampkin,
Doctoral Candidate,
Georgia State University

"Dr. Roman-Oliver's timely book applies new ideas regarding student engagement and inclusivity within existing dialogues of education and critical consciousness. Along with her collaborators, she offers several practical suggestions for utilizing Culturally Relevant Pedagogy in science classrooms and demonstrates the adaptability of these lesson plans to make them relevant for your own students."

Stephanie Opperman,
Associate Professor of History,
Georgia College and State University

Dr. Roman-Oliver masterfully tackles an important, yet underemphasized facet of Culturally Relevant Science Education. As educators, we are all familiar with the terminology. But how can we effectively implement this pedagogical model in an ever-changing classroom filled with diverse personalities and needs? *The Science I Know: Culturally Relevant Science Lessons from the Secondary Classrooms* explores the importance of cultural relevancy and how to implement this teaching and learning framework. With standards-based lessons that can be adapted to fit the diverse needs of any secondary science classroom, this book is a must read for all science teachers and teacher educators!

Dionne Lazenby, PhD

After 25 years of preparing middle and high school teachers, I have learned that they are far more likely to implement new concepts when they are able to see high quality, practical examples from similar classrooms. It is for this reason that I believe *The Science I Know: Culturally Relevant Science Lessons from Secondary Classrooms* can have a substantial impact on the quantity and quality of culturally relevant teaching in our nation's science classrooms. I highly recommend this inspiring book to both teacher educators preparing novice science teachers and to veteran teachers who are striving to meet the needs of ALL their students.

Cynthia Alby, PhD,
Author of Learning that matters:
A field guide to course design for transformative education

THE SCIENCE I KNOW

THE SCIENCE I KNOW

Culturally Relevant Science Lessons from Secondary Classrooms

BY SUZANNA ROMAN-OLIVER

Myers Education Press

Gorham, Maine

Myers
Education
Press

Published by Myers Education Press, LLC
P.O. Box 424
Gorham, ME 04038

Myers Education Press is an academic publisher specializing in books, e-books and digital content in the field of education. All of our books are subjected to a rigorous peer review process and produced in compliance with the standards of the Council on Library and Information Resources.

Library of Congress Cataloging-in-Publication Data available from Library of Congress.

13-digit ISBN 978-1-9755-0608-7 (paperback)
13-digit ISBN 978-1-9755-0609-4 (library networkable e-edition)
13-digit ISBN 978-1-9755-0610-0 (consumer e-edition)

Printed in the United States of America.

All first editions printed on acid-free paper that meets the American National Standards Institute Z39-48 standard.

Books published by Myers Education Press may be purchased at special quantity discount rates for groups, workshops, training organizations and classroom usage. Please call our customer service department at 1-800-232-0223 for details.

Cover design by Teresa Lagrange

Visit us on the web at **www.myersedpress.com** to browse our complete list of titles.

Contents

Acknowledgments

I AM GRATEFUL TO GOD FOR everything, for who He is, and for planting the dream of writing a book in my heart, almost 5 years ago.

Thank you to my wonderful husband, Bing, for being with me through every step of the journey, from the writing of the proposal, for which he lovingly provided feedback, to the final revisions. Thank you for loving me through it all and doing it so well.

To my son, Adrian, for celebrating this accomplishment with me and for teaching me so much about myself.

Thank you to my family for their unwavering support.

A special thank you to Cynthia Alby for being the first one to encourage me to write this book and for seeing its potential. Thank you, Chris Myers, for the opportunity to make my dream come true.

This book would not have been possible without the contribution of all the science teachers that embody culturally relevant pedagogy in their practice. Each of you understand that students are not blank slates and that when we draw on *the science they know*, learning can truly happen.

Many thanks to the education faculty at Georgia College and State University, for being excellent role models, especially to my department chair, Joanne Previts.

Finally, thank you to every former science education student and current science teacher that voiced their frustration about not finding a book that had standards-based lessons that implemented culturally relevant practices in the science classroom. You were the inspiration for this book. I hope we did a good job at filling that gap.

Introduction

DURING MOST OF MY 12 years teaching science to English Language Learners, I felt less than adequate. This was not a reflection of my science content knowledge. My undergraduate degree in biology positioned me as an expert in this and other science disciplines. It was also not a reflection of my pedagogical skills. I aimed at designing hands-on, cognitively challenging learning experiences that invited students to use problem-solving, engage in discussions, and collaborate towards a common goal. This feeling was due to the difficulties I experienced connecting students' background knowledge and culture to the concepts and ideas covered in class. As a teacher, I always tried to find out what my students knew about a topic before we dove into it. I was interested in their background knowledge in science. It was always fascinating to hear their ideas. However, drawing on students' previous knowledge is not the same as unveiling the connections to the bigger picture, the links to their cultural background and upbringing. There was a wealth of cultural knowledge in my students that I simply did not learn to tap into until much later in my teaching career.

After my initial years in academia, I realized that I was not alone in this. Through my research, it became evident that science teachers struggle with making these connections or finding good examples of how this looks in the classroom. Sure, they learn the theories and mostly understand the frameworks related to the role of culture in teaching and learning. However, bridging the gap between the theory and practice was a challenge.

The idea for *The Science I Know* originated during the completion of my PhD studies. My dissertation, titled *Culturally relevant science: A multiple case-study on the beliefs, experiences and practices of pre-service teachers in racially and ethnically diverse classrooms*, explored, among other things, how a group of seven pre-service science teachers incorporated the ideas of Ladson-Billings' Culturally Relevant Pedagogy (CRP) in their classrooms (Roman, 2019). The premise was that, knowing that these teachers were exposed to the different theories on multicultural education, including CRP, during their graduate studies, I was bound to find some examples in their practice.

I observed this group of teachers twice each month during a full academic year. Among the findings, it was clear that while they utilized many strategies to promote academic success, they had difficulty including activities that developed cultural competence and critical consciousness (I dive into each of these tenets of CRP in Chapter 3 of this book). It was interesting to further tap into their understanding of these areas as well, as part of the pre- and post-interviews I conducted. For some of them, these tenets or concepts were not very clear. Many of them expressed that they would like to incorporate these ideas more, but they struggled with picturing "what it looked like" in the science classroom. They referred to some of the articles they explored in their previous courses and talked about great examples of how to integrate CRP in language arts and social studies. However, they deemed science as too technical or objective, perhaps devoid of "culture."

The Science I Know is an answer to this. These are lessons from current science teachers created for their students. The purpose of this book is to showcase ways in which a group of teachers has taken into consideration students' ideas related to a topic, and has incorporated these into their planning to maximize students' funds of knowledge in the process. The lesson plans purposely follow the 5E framework, as I believe this to be an ideal sequencing for fostering inquiry-based learning in the science classroom. The lesson plans are also aligned to the Next Generation Science Standards to guide teachers in identifying the academic content and scientific skills that are targeted through the activities. Finally, a section discussing how the tenets of Culturally Relevant Pedagogy (Ladson-Billings, 1995) are addressed through the lesson is included. While some of these connections may seem obvious, I believed it was important to be explicit about their integration. It may also serve as a motivation to be intentional about aligning your lessons to the CRP goals.

References

Ladson-Billings, G. (1995). But that's just good teaching! The case for culturally relevant pedagogy. *Theory Into Practice, 34*(3), 159–165.

Roman, S. (2019). *Culturally relevant science: A multiple case-study on the beliefs, experiences and practices of pre-service teachers in racially and ethnically diverse classrooms* [Doctoral dissertation, Georgia State University]. ScholarWorks.

PART I

SETTING THE STAGE

ONE

The Shifting Role of Science Education

If you ask any science teacher about the ways science education has changed in the last few decades, they would probably have much to say. Although many shifts have occurred in this area, asking students that question may not yield the same result. Of course, we are familiar with how much time it takes for research findings to impact practice. I think most of us would agree that even the idea of incorporating students' culture into our teaching is relatively new, even when research and literature on multicultural education spans at least six decades (Banks, 1989). I recently had a conversation with a doctoral student who shared that one of the teachers at her school was asking questions about the "sudden" focus on culture in the classroom. While interest in the impact of culture in the classroom may have been spurred by civil rights struggles in the 60s, the evolution of multicultural education has been influenced by many social changes that have followed these events, especially immigration (Gorski, 1999). Gorski notes:

> Meanwhile, the cultural landscape of the United States continued to become less visibly white Christian and more visibly rich with cultural, racial, ethnic, and religious diversity, underscoring the necessity for everyone to develop a set of skills and knowledge that the present system was failing to provide all students. These included creative and critical thinking skills, intercultural competence, and social and global awareness. The education system was not only plagued by unequal treatment of traditionally oppressed groups, but was also ill-equipped to prepare even the most highly privileged students to competently participate in an increasingly diverse society. (Gorski, 1999)

In the next few pages, I would like to discuss some of the changes to the goals of science education, and as a result, its classroom practices. Then, I will briefly explore the role of equity within these new goals.

Early reforms in science education were the result of a report from the

National Commission on Excellence in Education. The report, *A Nation at Risk*, examined "the quality of education in the United States" in order to suggest "practical recommendations for educational improvement" (National Commission on Excellence in Education, 1983, p. 7). In reviewing the report, it is interesting to see how they referred to the education practices of that time as an "act of unthinking, unilateral educational disarmament" (p. 9). The following quote is powerful and further explains this statement:

> If an unfriendly foreign power had attempted to impose on America the mediocre educational performance that exists today, we might well have viewed it as an act of war. As it stands, we have allowed this to happen to ourselves. We have even squandered the gains in student achievement made in the wake of the Sputnik challenge. Moreover, we have dismantled essential support systems which helped make those gains possible. (p. 9)

Needless to say, the results of the report spurred the need for change in the ways we view the goals of education altogether, but also challenged us to rethink the role of science teaching specifically. The rest of the report goes on to present data from studies about students' performance in different areas to support this argument. Interestingly, only one of their sections summarizes data related to science, which in this case focuses on achievement scores on national assessments.

Several reform documents were created as a result of this report, including Science for All Americans, Benchmarks for Science Literacy, and National Science Education Standards (National Research Council, 2019). A few years later, the National Research Council developed a set of science standards for high school students that would become *A Framework for Science Education* (National Research Council, 2012), the predecessor of the Next Generation Science Standards (NGSS) that we are aligning our lesson plans to in the book. The Framework introduced three-dimensional learning or the 3Ds as a model to guide classroom instruction. These three dimensions are outlined and discussed further in Chapter 2 of this book.

Of course, what we are really intrigued about is how these changes impacted science education. While all three of the initial reform documents had a strong focus on scientific or science literacy, what this looked like varied. For the purpose of this book, we will use the following definition of science literacy from the National Science Education Standards (National Research Council, 1996): "Scientific literacy is the knowledge and understanding of scientific concepts and processes required for personal decision making, participation in civic and cultural affairs, and economic productivity" (p. 22). Furthermore:

> Scientific literacy means that a person can ask, find, or determine answers to questions derived from curiosity about everyday experiences. It means that a person has the ability to describe, explain, and predict natural phenomena. Scientific literacy entails being able to read with understanding articles about science in the popular press and to engage in social conversation about the validity of the conclusions. Scientific literacy implies that a person can identify scientific issues underlying national and local decisions and express positions that are scientifically and technologically informed. A literate citizen should be able to evaluate the quality of scientific information on the basis of its source and the methods used to generate it. Scientific literacy also implies the capacity to pose and evaluate arguments based on evidence and to apply conclusions from such arguments appropriately. (p. 22)

Recall your experiences as a student learning science. If I asked you how well this definition and these skills represent your own journey as a science learner, what would you say? Unfortunately, a lot of the science education that we were exposed to as students does not exactly align with these ideas.

When we read about the skills that are characteristic of a scientifically literate individual, we are compelled to think about the nature of science (NSTA, 2020). In other words, these are skills that all scientists should possess. I believe we can say that, in essence, the goals of science education evolved to ensure that students were developing their identities as scientists. Scientific identity is a broad field of research in science education. However, it is worth discussing it, even if briefly, as it relates to students from minority groups. Vincent-Ruz and Schunn (2018) described identity as "a multicomponent construct through which people internalize experiences, their context, see themselves as members of social groups, and intersect with their personal characteristic" (p. 9). In their research study, examining science identity in 7th and 9th graders, they concluded that both personal and external factors seem to contribute to students' science identities. When examining students' attitudes in the science class and even their motivations to pursue science-related careers, science identity seemed to be a strong indicator. Considering the academic performance, as well as the representation of minority groups in STEM fields, this is an important area of research for scholars focusing on culturally relevant pedagogy. Based on the findings from some of the literature reviewed, we could conclude that many of the science reform documents included goals of helping all students see themselves as scientists.

What about equity? What role does it play in the midst of these changes? The National Research Council, in their publication *A Framework for K-12 Science Education: Practices, Crosscutting Concepts, and Core Ideas*, states that "when people enter into the practices of science or engineering, they do not leave their cultural worldviews at the door. Instruction that fails to recognize this reality can adversely affect student engagement in science" (National Research Council, 2012, p. 284). This is a powerful statement that acknowledges the strong connection between culture and science identity. We rely on teachers that understand this and embody it in the way they plan, deliver, and assess instruction. Equity is defined in different ways by many scholars. For the purpose of this chapter, we use the definition of equity from the Next Generation Science Standards. Their publication *NGSS For All Students* focuses on the "importance of providing all students with high-quality science education" (Lee et al., 2015). In this sense, the standards are meant to ensure that all students, regardless of their race, ethnicity, gender, or socio-economic status, experience science instruction that exceeds expectations.

The National Research Council identifies two major sources of inequity related to science education: school/district inequities and "alienating" approaches to instruction (2012, p. 279). While we, as teachers, may not have direct control over the lack of resources or the number of high-quality teachers, we have the ability to structure learning experiences that invite all students and capitalize on their cultural knowledge. In other words, we have the power to minimize or eliminate approaches to instruction that are alienating students from certain groups. Among the council's recommendations for doing this are the following:

a) Make the learning relevant to students' context. The National Research Council states that "What counts as learning and what types of knowledge are seen as important are closely tied to a community's values and what is useful in that community context" (p. 284). I believe this goes beyond mere relevance, however. The activities that students engage in should have goals that reflect needs in their communities. This increases the value that students place in it, as it is not just about what the teacher says or the school wants, but about something that will benefit them and their families. Angela Calabrese Barton, in her book *Teaching Science for Social Justice* dives into this idea. She explains that truly enacting science for all involves "understanding in new ways the resources to which youth have access within any given science space, and the ways in which they may activate those resources to craft a science practice that meets their needs." (Barton, 2003, p. 118) This idea is clearly linked to the concept of critical consciousness explored further in Chapter 3 of this book.

b) Acknowledge and utilize students' discourse practices. "Recognizing that language and discourse patterns vary across culturally diverse groups, researchers point to the importance of accepting, even encouraging, students' classroom use of informal or native language and familiar modes of interaction" (National Academies of Sciences, Engineering, and Medicine. (2012). *A framework for K-12 science education: Practices, crosscutting concepts, and core ideas*. Washington, DC: The National Academies Press. https://doi.org/10.17226/13165, p. 285). This could refer to both students' home language or youth discourse patterns. Teachers can find connections between students' native discourse and scientific practices in order to facilitate the transition into using academic language. While it is common for science teachers to present vocabulary before a unit, Brown (2021) stresses the importance of introducing concepts before important vocabulary and allowing students to make sense of these using their own discourse patterns. The teacher can then introduce the vocabulary within the context of the topics after the conceptual understanding has developed.

c) Building on students' interest and identity. This relates to my previous point about the goal of developing students' scientific identity in the classroom. The power of such an approach is that, while it is important for all learners, "the benefits are particularly salient for those who would feel disenfranchised or disconnected from science should instruction neglect their personal inclinations" (National Research Council, 2012, p. 287).

d) Incorporating funds of knowledge. We will explore this concept further, but it is worth noting that some of the knowledge accumulated by certain groups may not align with the science principles and practices that are part of the goals of science education. However, teachers can find out and be intentional about incorporating those values that are aligned to these learning goals. When I talk to my future teachers about funds of knowledge, I like to refer to it as students' expertise. I often tell them about how much I would learn from my own students during my years as a science teacher. Their excitement to share about what they knew and to realize that this could be helpful in the science class was always inspiring. In order to truly maximize this practice, however, teachers need to be intentional about getting to know their students, their interests, and the things that they are passionate about. In the last chapter of this book, we look at ways in which we can do this.

In addition to these recommendations for making science inclusive, the Frameworks' publication suggests that teachers "Make Diversity Visible," which refers to acknowledging and displaying the contributions of diverse cultural groups to science, and "Value Multiple Modes of Expression," which stresses the importance of how students may demonstrate understanding of ideas in different ways. Making diversity visible goes beyond showcasing scientists from underrepresented groups and their contributions. It entails scrutinizing and revising the curriculum materials and assessment practices to ensure that it is representative of all students and not just the majority. Valuing multiple modes of expression involves reflecting on our assessment practices as well. As the publication states, "exemplary assessment practice recognizes that there are multiple ways in which students might express their developing understanding, although not all forms of assessment allow for such multiple modes of expression" (p. 289).

Most recent scientific reforms and curricular changes have been powered partly by the low performance of students from underrepresented groups. Therefore, incorporating students' culture in the science classroom has become an important part of teaching preparation programs. In part, this falls under a greater umbrella of addressing the needs of *all* students (a.k.a., differentiation). However, teachers' difficulties with connecting, building relationships, and reaching students from diverse backgrounds may be the steam powering this change engine.

References

Banks, J. (1989). Multicultural education: Characteristics and goals. In J. Banks & C. Banks (Eds.), *Multicultural education: Issues and perspectives*. Boston: Allyn and Bacon.

Barton, A. C. (2003). *Teaching science for social justice*. (p. 118). Teachers College Press.

Brown, B. A. (2021). *Science in the city: Culturally relevant STEM education*. Harvard Education Press.

Gorski, P. C. (1999, November). *A brief history of multicultural education*. EdChange. http://www.edchange.org/multicultural/papers/edchange_history.html

Lee, O., Miller, E., & Januszyk, R. (2015). *NGSS for all students*. NSTA Press.

National Commission on Excellence in Education. (1983). *A nation at risk: The imperative for educational reform*. https://edreform.com/wp-content/uploads/2013/02/A_Nation_At_Risk_1983.pdf

National Research Council. (1996). *National science education standards*. The National Academies Press. https://doi.org/10.17226/4962

National Research Council. (2012). *A framework for K-12 science education: Practices, crosscutting concepts, and core ideas*. The National Academies Press. https://doi.org/10.17226/13165

National Research Council. (2019). *Science and engineering for grades 6-12: Investigation and design at the center*. The National Academies Press. https://doi.org/10.17226/25216

NSTA. (2020, January). *Position statement-Nature of science*. https://www.nsta.org/nstas-official-positions/nature-science

Vincent-Ruz, P., & Schunn, C. D. (2018). The nature of science identity and its role as the driver of student choices. *International Journal of STEM Education, 5*(4). https://doi.org/10.1186/s40594-018-0140-5

TWO

The 5E Instructional Model and the Next Generation Science Standards

THE 5E INSTRUCTIONAL MODEL HAS been implemented in science classrooms for decades. BSCS developed the 5E model as part of a design study funded by IBM (Bybee et al., 2006). The model draws from the SCIS learning cycle (Lawson et al., 1989). The 5E model promotes inquiry and follows the premise that teachers need to start from where their students are, cognitively speaking, and address prior knowledge and preconceptions before beginning instruction. The 5E model encourages exploration of topics and collaboration that foster discussions and may lead to the use of argumentative practices. All these are skills that are also outlined in science reform documents. These also align with the tenets of academic success and cultural competence, as described by Ladson-Billings' Culturally Relevant Pedagogy theory.

The 5Es are: Engage, Explore, Explain, Elaborate, and Evaluate. The goal of the first phase is to "engage" students into the content at the start of the class. The teacher may begin the lesson with a scientific phenomenon, a puzzling question, or a startling scenario, for instance. Ideally, the teacher will use something that is relevant to students and allows for connections to be made between past experiences and the content. This is also an opportunity to check on students' understanding of a concept. Additionally, it allows teachers to discover misconceptions that students may hold about the topic. In science, an example of an "engage" could be a demonstration in which the outcome is unexpected or a short video clip that asks students to hypothesize or reflect on a scientific process. One of my favorite ones to present to future teachers is the "boat-in-pool" puzzler from pbs.org (2000). In this brain-teaser, students are asked to hypothesize what will happen to the level of water if a rock that has been sitting in a boat inside a pool is dropped into the water. I typically ask students to collaborate to write a hypothesis and then share it with the class with their explanation.

The next phase, "explore," requires students to use concrete experiences to dive into the ideas from the previous phase. As Bybee et al. notes, "Engagement brings about disequilibrium; exploration initiates the process of equilibration" (2006, p. 9). Here, the author is referring to cognitive disequilibrium and equilibrium. In other words, students are exposed to a problem or situation during the "engage" that they will need to work to solve during the exploration. It is recommended that students participate in hands-on activities at this time. Alternatively, teachers may use online activities to explore "objects, events or situations" (PBS, 2000, p. 9). The teacher acts as a facilitator during the process and guides students throughout the exploration or investigation of the problem, case, or phenomenon. Laboratory experiments and online simulations are great ways to engage students in testing out their ideas.

In the "boat-in-pool" activity, I provide large and small plastic containers, as well as rocks, and ask students to model the situation. They place water in the large container and then place the small container inside of it. They place rocks inside the small container and mark the level of water. Then, they carefully proceed to drop the rocks in the water, making sure that it does not splash. This is also a great opportunity to practice skills related to designing experiments and to discuss experimental error in context. As a facilitator, I ask them to design a plan to test their hypothesis, before they are provided the materials, of course. Once they start, they record their observations. Many of them replicate the experiment as well.

The third phase, "explain," allows for students to be exposed to the terms, concepts, and processes that are related to the "engage" and "explore" experiences they just participated in. The teacher should initiate this phase by giving students an opportunity to explain or discuss their findings and observations from the previous phase. After this, the teacher presents the scientific processes and concepts using the findings from the exploration. This allows for the introduction of new vocabulary in a way that is contextual, as opposed to disconnected from real life or their experiences. In the example of the boat-in-pool puzzler, I allow each group to describe what they observed. I also give them an opportunity to discuss how these findings relate to their hypothesis and to explain why it aligns to it or not. In my past experience working with students and science teachers, this part can be somewhat difficult. Students are hesitant to admit that they are wrong and some may label the experiment as flawed at times. It may be important to use this as an opportunity to discuss the nature of science. After students have a chance to share their thoughts, I proceed to provide an explanation for the phenomenon. The concepts of density, buoyancy, and volume are reviewed. Students are also encouraged to review their initial explanations for their hypotheses.

The next phase, "elaborate," allows for the extension and transfer of the concepts learned during the previous three phases. In other words, students are presented with different scenarios in which they need to apply the concepts or skills learned. Ideally, students will have an opportunity to collaborate and listen to other students' ideas during this time. However, the "elaborate" can also be used to further research the concepts explored or ask different questions related to the exploration.

When I do the boat-in-pool activity, I ask my students to think about something they would change about the materials or about the steps they followed to test their hypothesis. They sometimes do research to better understand the concepts explored and consider ways in which different materials may be used. It is interesting to see them wonder about how the type of rock or its shape may make a difference in the outcome. They also wonder if the shape of the small container or the amount of water in the larger container may change the result. I encourage them to test these ideas and discuss the results. When I do this activity with science teachers, I ask them to consider real-life applications for the concepts that were explored and to design an "elaborate" activity that their students could complete.

Finally, the "evaluate" phase gives students an opportunity to receive feedback on their learning. Although evaluation may occur throughout the sequence, teachers may formally assess students at the end to determine if they have reached the learning goals set. Pre-assessment of students' conceptions can occur when they are drawing hypotheses in the "engage." This can also reveal misconceptions that need to be addressed during the learning sequence. Formative assessment may be conducted in the form of questions asked during the "explore" and by evaluating students' responses during the "explain." The "elaborate" can be used to assess the ability of students to apply or transfer the learning to new situations. In the boat-in-pool activity, all these forms of assessment are integrated, either informally or formally.

Why did I choose this model? The 5E Instructional Model has been incorporated with success for decades across school districts in the United States. The model is effective at designing learning experiences that are inquiry-based and engaging (Duran & Duran, 2004). It has become a staple in curriculum design and science teacher preparation programs across the nation and beyond. I have incorporated the model both as a teacher and as a professor. To this date, no other science teaching model has been researched and evaluated so extensively. A report prepared for the Office of Science Education at the National Institutes of Health summarized the following data (Bybee et al., 2006):

> In spring 2006, [a simple internet] search showed the following range of uses: more than 235,000 lesson plans developed and implemented using the BSCS 5E Instructional Model; more than 97,000 posted and discrete examples of universities using the 5E model in their course syllabi; more than 73,000 examples of curriculum materials developed using the 5E model; more than 131,000 posted and discrete examples of teacher education programs or resources that use the 5Es; and at least three states that strongly endorse the 5E model, including Texas, Connecticut, and Maryland. (p. 1)

The 5E Instructional Model was the clear choice when considering how to structure the lessons for this book. Most of the teachers that contributed lesson plans either currently use this model or have been formally exposed to it through their undergraduate or graduate degrees (some are former students). The model also aligns well with the principles of culturally relevant pedagogy as it starts by engaging students in the content through the use of relevant examples, phenomena, or questions that are thought provoking. These provide an opportunity for students to share their previous knowledge and background before exposure to the learning activities. The "explain" stage also prioritizes students' interpretations of the discovery experiences, promoting student agency before the vocabulary and concepts are presented. The "elaborate" section facilitates the application of new concepts learned, an important cognitive skill that is associated with higher-order thinking. This could be an opportunity for students to analyze case studies or community issues that affect them, making room for critical consciousness to develop.

The decision to use the Next Generation Science Standards (NGSS) to address academic success takes into account its rigorous development and effectiveness throughout the last decades in education. The NGSS were developed by 26 states and a team of writers that included teachers, scientists, and education researchers. They are based on the *A Framework for K-12 Science Education* report by the National Research Council (2012). The NGSS underwent several cycles of review leading to their publication in 2013 (NGSS,

2013). Currently, 44 states have either adopted the standards or developed standards based on their framework (Barrett-Zahn, 2023). The quality of the standards and their successful implementation across the nation positions it as the measuring stick for science education. The use of the standards across all different grade levels has been extensively researched since their publication. It has proven to be an effective framework for engaging science students in high-quality learning that promotes collaboration, problem-solving, and discovery.

My goal is for this book to be applicable to science teachers across all states. Therefore, choosing the NGSS as a framework to analyze the potential of the lessons to promote higher-order thinking skills was important. The NGSS framework organizes science learning into three main dimensions: 1) cross-cutting concepts; 2) science and engineering practices; and 3) disciplinary core ideas. "Cross-cutting concepts" refers to ideas that are explored in all science disciplines, such as "cause and effect" or "systems." "Science and engineering practices" refer to the specific skills that relate to doing science. In other words, these refer to how scientists conduct investigations or do inquiry. Examples of these practices are developing models or engaging in argumentation. Finally, "disciplinary core ideas" refer to the specific content or topics that are part of each scientific discipline. For instance, a student completing a life science course should be exposed to the concept of interactions and energy flow in ecosystems. In the same way, a student in a physical science course should engage in activities that demonstrate how forces interact to produce a change in motion. The corresponding areas for each of these dimensions are identified within all the lesson plans featured. Not only are the specific concepts, practices, and core ideas a part of each lesson, but their alignment to academic success, as described by CRP, is discussed as well. This is intended to guide teachers in seeing the connection between the lesson and the content and skills that are required by students at each grade level.

References

Barrett-Zahn, E. (2023). Ten years of NGSS: Where are we now? *Science and Children*, *60*(4), 6-6.

Bybee, R., Taylor, J., Gardner, A., Van Scotter, P., Carson Powell, J., Westbrook, A., & Landes, N. (2006). *The BSCS 5E instructional model: Origins and effectiveness*. BSCS Science Learning. https://bscs.org/reports/the-bscs-5e-instructional-model-origins-and-effectiveness/

Duran, L. B., & Duran, E. (2004). The 5E instructional model: A learning cycle approach for inquiry-based science teaching. *Science Education Review, 3*(2), 49–58.

Lawson, A. E., Abraham, M. R., & Renner, J. W. (1989). *A theory of instruction: Using the learning cycle to teach science concepts and thinking skills.* National Association for Research in Science Teaching.

National Research Council. (2012). *A framework for K-12 science education: Practices, crosscutting concepts, and core ideas.* The National Academies Press. https://doi.org/10.17226/13165

NGSS Lead States. (2013). *Next Generation Science Standards: For states, by states.* The National Academies Press.

PBS. (2000, November). *NOVA online-boat-in-pool puzzler.* https://www.pbs.org/wgbh/nova/lasalle/buoypool.html

THREE

Why Culturally Relevant Pedagogy?

In the last few decades, many frameworks have focused on restructuring the way teachers approach culture in the classroom. Culturally relevant pedagogy (CRP) was the result of several years of research studies focused on strategies used by teachers of African-American students (Ladson-Billings, 1995). Ladson-Billings identified practices among these teachers that made them effective when working with these students and contributed to developing their academic success, cultural competence, and critical consciousness.

When describing academic success, Ladson-Billings stressed the importance of students achieving excellence, as measured by the school's standards. The teachers observed were intentional about identifying the academic needs of students and helping them reach their learning goals. As she concluded, it was not just about getting good grades, but about "students [choosing] academic excellence" (p. 160). In science, this could be observed as students meeting the standards, whether these are the Next Generation Science Standards (NGSS), state, or district-specific ones.

As a discipline, science goes beyond the knowledge or comprehension of the content, of course. Students should be able to display the skills and practices that allow them to be effective participants in the scientific community. For example, if a student is able to write the equation for photosynthesis, but is unable to design an experiment to determine how the acidity in the soil affects the process, the student has mastered that content but not necessarily the scientific practices that relate to it. Since many states have either adopted or utilized the NGSS to design their standards, this is what we used when addressing academic success within the lessons. While the lessons address different content standards (or core ideas), the scientific practices and cross-cutting concepts can be applied to different topics, as well as all science disciplines. For instance, a student that struggles with analyzing and interpreting data from a graph about the growth of a population may have similar difficulties when facing a graph representing the speed of a vehicle over time (i.e., scientific practice = "Analyzing and interpreting data"). In the same way, a student that understands the law of conservation of energy from the perspective of chemical reactions should be able to apply this when analyzing how energy is lost across trophic levels in a food chain (i.e., cross-cutting concept = “Energy and Matter: Flows, Cycles, and Conservation”). (National Research Council, 2012).

Beyond the goal of academic success, CRP aims at building cultural competence, which is equated to maintaining “cultural integrity” (Ladson-Billings, 1995, p. 160). In other words, a learning environment that embodies culturally relevant pedagogy not only allows students to be authentic, but encourages it, as the teacher sees the value of the unique attributes that each culture brings to the classroom. Additionally, students’ culture is, as Ladson-Billings notes, “a vehicle” and a “bridge” for learning (p. 161). In other words, it connects students’ lives at home with the classroom learning experiences.

In her article “But that’s just good teaching! The case for culturally relevant pedagogy,” Ladson-Billings suggests several ways of developing cultural competence in the classroom. For instance, teachers could use students’ music or youth culture interest to build lessons that capitalize on their knowledge of these. As an example, one of my former Art Education students incorporated K-Pop in one of her drawing lessons, because of its popularity among students. She allowed students to change their drawings, however, to include elements that aligned better with their own unique physical features (e.g., hair-styles, skin-tones, etc.). Another strategy mentioned is to use parents as knowledgeable resources in the classroom. The article refers to these experiences as “residencies” that parents engage in to teach a skill to students. These can range from baking or cooking to sports and skilled trades. In this sense, the concept of cultural competence goes hand in hand with *funds of knowledge* (Vélez-Ibáñez & Greenberg, 1992). Vélez-Ibáñez and Greenberg identified cultural practices that are necessary for the survival of households of US–Mexican families. They coined these “funds of knowledge,” or the knowledge and skills that these families have formed, learned, and transmitted to their children to ensure their well-being through generations (p. 314). Some examples of these funds were practices related to cooking, childcare, agriculture, and religion. The idea that these funds have been transferred from generation to generation also aligns with most common definitions of culture. When teachers are able to mine students’ “funds of knowledge,” there is a greater chance to incorporate these in the classroom, which aligns to the concept of cultural competence. The more teachers incorporate these funds, the greater the relevance of the topics discussed with students' lives. In a sense, the teacher is able to *bridge* what students are learning in the classroom with what they are experiencing at home.

Building cultural competence can also be observed when allowing students to use forms of discourse that may not be considered traditional. For example, one of the teachers in Ladson-Billings' study allowed students to write and speak using nonstandard English, while they progressed towards standard forms of the language. A similar example would be seen in students being able to use their native languages when writing an essay to facilitate the flow of ideas. Students could later translate these to English before submitting their final work. This was a practice that I utilized often when teaching English Language Learners.

In my past experience working with science teachers, I have seen lessons that demonstrate an effort to promote students' cultural competence. For example, one of my former teacher candidates designed a lesson in which students explored the Zika virus epidemic in different countries. They looked at data and analyzed the prevalence of the disease in these areas. Since many of her students were from Brazil, they were able to contribute to the discussion with their cultural knowledge about weather, habitats, and practices related to the infection and propagation of the virus. Because of the impact that the epidemic had specifically on birth control, the students were able to share their values related to this as well (Lowe et al., 2018). These contributions proved to enrich the discussions and benefit all students involved. Exposure to other cultures is an important aspect of cultural competence as well. Additionally, the teacher became a learner through the exchange of ideas. This is a clear example of how the science content that students are learning can connect directly to, and draw from, their experiences.

Finally, an important goal of CRP is that students are able to develop critical consciousness as part of their learning experiences. Ladson-Billings defined critical consciousness as the ability to "critique the cultural norms, values, mores, and institutions that produce and maintain social inequities" (p. 162). For example, students may be given the opportunity in class to express their views on and critique the information within their textbooks or the lack of resources in their schools. Students may also be engaged in social action efforts to address issues in their community.

When I completed my dissertation research, my findings suggested that most science teachers struggled with identifying elements of or implementing critical consciousness in their classrooms. While Ladson-Billings' studies include several examples of this area in English language arts and social studies, examples in science across the literature are limited. Other scholars have looked into how to implement this tenet in science, however. Barton (2003) explored the experiences of teachers and students in an after-school program. These are documented in the book *Teaching Science for Social Justice*. Among other things, the researchers observed that among students from families of low socioeconomic status, the motivation to engage in science activities increases when they are able to utilize their leadership skills to engage in projects and design things that will add value to their lives and communities. In her book, Barton discussed how educators need to reconceptualize their ideas about barriers or challenges to students' learning as assets (p. 29). This entails teachers exercising critical consciousness as well. The students in the study developed critical consciousness in many areas—Two particularly stand out. Firstly, students were critical about "the social arrangements that determined participation in science, rules that determined what actions were allowable, and opportunities to learn and do real science" (p. 89). In reference to this, the youth in the study expressed frustration about the way their teachers were teaching them science and how it seemed that they were provided "watered down" content and assignments. Secondly, they were critical about what it means to *do science* and sought to find ways to use science to solve issues that were concerning them.

Upadhyay et al. (2020) also explored critical consciousness in high school students. They concluded that when it is used in science education it can "cultivate civic engagement that promotes social change actions" (p. 1141). Just as in Barton's study, Upadhyay et al. observed that students "from marginalized groups ... are capable of making connections between science content and sociopolitical issues that matter to them" (p. 1141). Finally, their research suggests that these students can use science to engage in social action that builds "awareness related to structural, social, political, and curricular issues that have had detrimental effects on them in their communities" (p.1141). Their study focused on an Indigenous group, Tharu, and their engagement in activities focused on water as a resource. Throughout the unit, students also explored sickle-cell anemia and its prevalence in their communities.

The students became critical of issues surrounding water access and how this impacted their hygiene practices, for instance. Additionally, they questioned health practices related to caring for individuals in their community with sickle-cell disease. In another research study, Upadhyay et al., (2020) argue that tapping into critical consciousness can be done by leveraging "science contents supporting students to critically explore sociocultural and sociopolitical issues that they encounter in the community" (p. 70). Their research explored how students engaged in critical reflection and discussions about issues of racial and social discrimination, both in the ELA and science classroom.

Marosi et al., notes that there is only one study focused on science education that has reported "students' outcomes with respect to the three tenets of CRP" (2021, p. 147). The study they are referring to is Laughter and Adams (2012). During my dissertation research, I also noticed that this was the only study that examined critical consciousness. The study was conducted with middle school students and focused on a lesson in which students discussed Derrick Bell's short story "The Space Traders." The teacher featured in the study utilized the text to "engage middle school students in thinking about bias in larger societal contexts and in their own lives" (p. 1019).

Despite the limited examples in science education literature, there is potential to develop critical consciousness through science topics. For instance, there are a plethora of examples that document the interplay between science and society. New science research and its technology applications can be discussed in the classroom through the lens of social issues, (i.e., poverty, discrimination, and healthcare). Using the lens of social justice, students can engage in discussions, write essays or letters, as well as participate in debates to analyze these issues and brainstorm solutions. Furthermore, using social justice as a lens can help students understand their role and identity as part of the scientific community. This becomes critical when we consider the limited representation of minorities in STEM:

> Minoritized youth can face dehumanization and marginalization in schooling on a daily basis. These oppressions are heightened in STEM education through the underpinning norms, routines, discourses, and practices of whiteness and heteropatriarchy. Not only do these norms define what it means to know, do, and become in STEM, they also shape what and how classrooms and communities interact in STEM education. (Xu et al., 2022, p. 22)

It is imperative that these conversations are not only a common part of science education, but that teachers are intentional about their goals when engaging students in these learning experiences.

Answering the question "Why culturally relevant pedagogy?" becomes easier when we consider the relevance of these goals in science education. First, we want to ensure all students have access to quality science teaching and that they are successful academically. This is not only a school goal, as it benefits our society and nation as a whole. We have already discussed in Chapter 1 what the alternative of this was in the 1980s. As teachers, we want science to be relevant to students. This is not possible without getting to know students, understanding what they already know, and using this information to craft the learning experiences. Cultural competence focuses on this. Students' daily experiences are significantly shaped by their culture and everyday lives. Finally, we want to ensure that students' engagement with science goes beyond memorization or hands-on activities that are disconnected from the "why" of it all. We want students that are able to identify problems and collaborate to design solutions. We want agents of change, not mere passive recipients of information. Critical consciousness is not only a worthy goal, it is necessary in a world that is constantly changing and is bombarded by misinformation. This will require individuals that are able to critique information, its sources, and make decisions that affect them and their communities.

References

Barton, A. C. (2003). *Teaching science for social justice.* Teachers College Press.

Ladson-Billings, G. (1995). But that's just good teaching! The case for culturally relevant pedagogy. *Theory Into Practice, 34*(3), 159–165.

Laughter, J. C., & Adams, A. D. (2012). Culturally relevant science teaching in middle school. *Urban Education, 47*(6), 1106–1134.

Lowe, R., Barcellos, C., Brasil, P., Cruz, O. G., Honório, N. A., Kuper, H., & Carvalho, M. S. (2018). The Zika virus epidemic in Brazil: from discovery to future implications. *International Journal of Environmental Research and Public Health, 15*(1), 96.

Marosi, N., Avraamidou, L., & Galani, L. (2021). Culturally relevant pedagogies in science education as a response to global migration. *SN Social Sciences, 1*(6), 147.

National Research Council. (2012). *A framework for K-12 science education: Practices, crosscutting concepts, and core ideas.* The National Academies Press. https://doi.org/10.17226/13165

Upadhyay, B., Atwood, E., & Tharu, B. (2020). Actions for sociopolitical consciousness in a high school science class: A case study of ninth grade class with predominantly Indigenous students. *Journal of Research in Science Teaching, 57*(7), 1119–1147.

Upadhyay, B., Coffino, K., Alberts, J., & Rummel, A. (2021). STEAM education for critical consciousness: Discourses of liberation and social change among sixth-grade students. *Asia-Pacific Science Education, 7*(1), 64–95.

Vélez-Ibáñez, C. G., & Greenberg, J. B. (1992). Formation and transformation of funds of knowledge among US-Mexican households. *Anthropology & Education Quarterly, 23*(4), 313–335.

Xu, G., Benavides, A., Calabrese-Barton, A., Tan, E., Bliesener, S., DiFrancesco, G., & Barton, S. C. (2022). Critical consciousness in engineering for sustainable communities: A justice-oriented approach connecting schools and communities. *Connected Science Learning, 4*(1).

FOUR

How to Use this Book

BEFORE I DELVE INTO MY recommendations in terms of how to make the most out of this book, I would like to address what this book is not. This book is not intended to be a prescribed set of lessons that you should implement in your classrooms "as is." In other words, while the lessons provide ideas that you could incorporate in your own classes, they are not meant to be "plugged in" without taking into consideration the students you teach and what they bring into the classroom. It does not introduce a new or different theoretical framework or model for incorporating culture in the classroom. Culturally relevant pedagogy has been around for decades and has been incorporated with success in classrooms across the nation.

If you are a teacher, my goal is that the lessons will serve as an inspiration for you to create learning experiences that draw from students' prior knowledge, expertise, and cultural capital. Each teacher featured in this book is from a different school, district, county, and even state. Each has a unique group of students and a distinctive set of challenges related to teaching these students. Each teacher has a different background, discipline expertise, and level of experience, along with the biases that these entail. What they do have in common, however, is a goal of becoming culturally relevant science teachers. They each share an understanding that students come to our classrooms with knowledge and skills that can be capitalized on, built on, and further developed. Finally, each teacher sees themselves as a learner in the classroom, as much, or perhaps more, than their students. Creating a culturally relevant classroom starts with the teacher's disposition. This is, albeit, the greatest challenge.

If you are a teacher educator, this book can serve as a resource to introduce culturally relevant pedagogy through the lens of science education. It will provide a role model for potential activities that engage future teachers in creating culturally relevant science lessons. Whenever I have my own students complete a similar assignment, the biggest question they ask is if there is an exemplar from previous courses that they may look at. The integration, as I mentioned earlier, is made explicit in each chapter to facilitate the connections with the different tenets. This connection of theory and practice is necessary for pre-service teachers and even in-service teachers that are just now being exposed to Ladson-Billings' ideas.

Again, while you should be able to incorporate the ideas in the lessons with ease, this does not mean that the learning will be relevant to the students you teach (again, because they were created for a unique group of students). I earnestly believe that this same caution should be taken when examining online lesson plans and deciding to adopt them in your classroom. As we often hear, what works with some may not work with others. When using this book, use the following questions to guide your planning:

- What are the goals I have for my students at the end of this lesson/unit?
- What important content, skills, and vocabulary is required of students? (i.e., standards/ academic success)
- What do I know about my students that will help me incorporate their cultural knowledge and skills into the lesson? (i.e., cultural competence)
- Are there opportunities to engage students beyond the content towards becoming critical about implications in their lives or communities? (i.e., critical consciousness)

As you read the lessons, you may find examples of practices that are similar to yours. The reality is that most teachers adapted common lesson plans in ways that would reflect the goals of the NGSS standards better, while trying to integrate students' culture in the process. You may even come up with new ideas or ways to revise these based on your students and their respective cultures. You may even be a bit skeptical about how the lessons reflect culturally relevant pedagogy. I am reminded of Ladson-Billings' first article "But that's just good teaching!" (1995). This is at the heart of CRP. It is good teaching, by great teachers!

References

Ladson-Billings, G. (1995). But that's just good teaching! The case for culturally relevant pedagogy. *Theory Into Practice*, *34*(3), 159–165.

PART II

CULTURALLY RELEVANT LESSONS

FIVE

Lessons from the Classroom

THE NEXT FEW SECTIONS CONTAIN lesson plans created by middle and high school pre-service and in-service teachers. Most of the teachers that contributed to this section are either current or former students of mine. The first five lessons have a biology or life science focus as they explore biodiversity, genetics, nutrients, and systems of the body. Any lesson targeted for a high school biology course can be easily adapted to a middle school life science course. I recommend identifying the appropriate NGSS 3D areas that better align to the content for your specific grade level before designing the activities, however.

The following three lessons feature energy changes and transfer. While they target different grade levels, the activities used can also be adapted for a lower or higher grade level. The last lesson (i.e., 5.9) in this section, however, is a genetics one aimed at middle school students. The lesson is featured here because it was written by the same contributor as lesson 5.8.

The structure of the lesson is the same throughout each section. At the beginning, you will find the title of the lesson as well as the grade level and science course targeted. Because all the lessons follow the 5E learning cycle, the suggested time for these varies but is not less than two regular class periods (i.e., 55–60 minutes). Many of the teachers featured teach block periods and have therefore created lessons that extend to 3-5 instructional hours. The lesson objectives and a brief description introduce the goals for the students as well as summarize some of the main activities that take place. Following this, I have included the 3D areas that align to the content and skills featured in the lesson (i.e., cross-cutting concepts, science and engineering practices, and disciplinary core ideas).

The lesson describes each of the 5Es in the learning cycle and includes references to articles, web resources, or videos that the teachers are incorporating throughout the lesson. You will notice that the "evaluate" stage describesthe many forms of evaluation that occur at different times during the lesson. Therefore, it will typically apply to multiple days of instructions. The section that follows, "Culturally Relevant Practices," discusses how the lesson aligns to the tenets in Ladson-Billings' framework (i.e., academic success, cultural competence, and critical consciousness). While most of the lessons feature a connection to critical consciousness, unfortunately it was not always possible to tie this area into the activities that students engaged in. In some lessons, there are suggestions for consideration related to how to integrate this area, however.

Although we have explored the concept of funds of knowledge as related to cultural competence, I decided to include a separate discussion of this at the end of the lesson. In this section, teachers described how they tapped into students' funds of knowledge during the lesson to enrich the learning experience for all. Finally, some important questions for teachers' consideration are included at the end. These are not comprehensive, but identify some areas within the lesson that may require further planning or preparation.

LESSON PLAN 5.1

Human Activities and Biodiversity

Tara Conner

Lesson Title
Human Activities and Biodiversity

Grade Level/Course
High School-Environmental Science

Suggested Time
Two 90-minute blocks

Learning Objectives

- Students will be able to describe examples of human activity that impact biodiversity in an ecosystem.
- Students will be able to compare and contrast different regions' practices in terms of their impact on biodiversity.

Description
This lesson introduces students to the concept of biodiversity and its connection with the health of an ecosystem. Students will explore cultural practices and human activities that can impact biodiversity. They will also have an opportunity to discuss how these cultural practices affect biodiversity and biodiversity conservation.

Next Generation Science Standards

Crosscutting Concepts

- Cause and effect
- Stability and change

Science and Engineering Practices

- Obtaining, evaluating, and communicating information
- Constructing explanations

Disciplinary Core Ideas

"LS4.D: Biodiversity and Humans—Humans depend on the living world for the resources and other benefits provided by biodiversity. But human activity is also having adverse impacts on biodiversity through overpopulation, overexploitation, habitat destruction, pollution, introduction of invasive species, and climate change. Thus, sustaining biodiversity so that ecosystem functioning and productivity are maintained is essential to supporting and enhancing life on Earth. Sustaining biodiversity also aids humanity by preserving landscapes of recreational or inspirational value." (National Research Council. 2012. *A Framework for K-12 Science Education: Practices, Crosscutting Concepts, and Core Ideas.* Washington, DC: The National Academies Press. https://doi.org/10.17226/13165, p. 166)

5E Lesson

Day 1

Engage

The teacher will begin the lesson by discussing biodiversity and the significance of biodiversity in maintaining a healthy ecosystem and supporting life. Students will be instructed to reflect on their own cultural backgrounds and how their communities interact with nature and ecosystems. Students will be informed that this lesson will explore how cultural practices and human activities can impact biodiversity and conservation efforts.

Students will be asked the following questions:

- What is biodiversity and why is it important for our planet and its ecosystems?
- Do you have any cultural practices or traditions that involve interaction with nature and the environment?
- Have you or your community ever been involved in conservation efforts? If so, what were they and what impact did they have?
- What are some ways human activities negatively impact biodiversity?

Explore

Students will be assigned to groups. Groups will be assigned a cultural or geographical region (i.e., Africa, Mexico, Arabic nations, United States, etc.). Students will research and identify factors that affect biodiversity in their assigned regions. Students will explore both positive and negative factors that impact biodiversity. They will use library resources, online sources,[1] and/or textbooks. The teacher will be walking around offering help in finding information and directing the research. Students will also be prompted to discuss and share their findings in their groups. Students will be asked to prepare a visual presentation of their findings. They will be free to choose the method they would like to use (e.g., PowerPoint, Google Slides, Book Creator, poster). Visual representation will highlight factors affecting biodiversity, including a brief explanation of how cultural practices and human activity influence biodiversity.

Day 2

Explain

Each group will present their findings to the class. Groups will be given 10 minutes to present. Each group member must speak during the presentation. After each presentation, the floor will be open for questions and discussion. The teacher will moderate time and assist with ending the presentation if necessary.

Elaborate

A discussion comparing and contrasting the factors affecting biodiversity in the different cultural/geographical regions will follow students' presentations. The importance of respecting and incorporating traditional ecological knowledge will be emphasized, along with how cultural practices can promote conservation. Students will be asked to write a brief reflection of the lesson answering the following questions: 1. How does culture impact biodiversity in different regions? 2. What are the positive and negative factors affecting biodiversity in the cultural/geographical region you researched? 3. How can cultural practices and indigenous knowledge promote biodiversity conservation? Alternatively, students could be asked to create an action plan outlining how they would promote biodiversity conservation in their own communities.

Evaluate

Students' understanding of the concept of biodiversity is pre-assessed at the start of the class through their responses to the introductory questions. The "explain" allows for the teacher to assess how well students have interpreted and organized the information they reviewed during the "explore." As students discuss the different factors that impact biodiversity, the teacher can ask questions to get clarification or check on their comprehension of the concept. Finally, students have an opportunity to summarize the learning experience through their reflection in the "elaborate" section.

Culturally Relevant Practices

Academic Success

This lesson entails students engaging in research activities as well as using library resources, online resources, and textbooks to gather information. Students are also asked to present the information in a visual format and engage in group discussion and class presentations. Students engage in research skills and the use of information literacy which promotes academic success in all areas, not only science. Through the use of group discussion and class presentations, students enhance their communication skills as well as their presentation skills and public speaking. The last part of this lesson encourages individual reflection which promotes self-awareness. Through reflective practices, students can take ownership of their learning by identifying their knowledge of the subject and also areas for improvement. By researching, presenting, and reflecting, students are developing critical thinking skills.

Cultural Competence

Throughout the lesson, students explore and discuss the impact of cultural practices and biodiversity. Because students are assigned specific cultural/geographical regions, they are exposed to varying cultural contexts, leading to an understanding of how cultural diversity can influence biodiversity. Students engage in a class discussion, sharing experiences and insights from different cultural backgrounds. This leads to an inclusive environment where student cultures are valued and respected. Through this lesson, students learn to recognize and appreciate the different cultural perspectives and knowledge that relates to ecosystems and biodiversity. Through their research, students come to appreciate how different cultures relate to the environment. Through sharing, students learn about other cultural perspectives and values which leads to students learning to respect other cultures and being open to other perspectives.

Critical Consciousness

This lesson encourages students to analyze factors that affect biodiversity as well as the implications of human activities in different cultural contexts. Students are instructed to include both positive and negative impacts. Through sharing, students are able to discuss their different perspectives and raise thought-provoking questions. By examining traditional ecological practices of the different cultures, students can develop an understanding of other ways of interacting with the environment and consider new ideas for biodiversity conservation. When students explore both positive and negative impacts of human activities on the environment, they become aware of the consequences of those activities. Students also become aware of the complexities and ethical magnitude of environmental issues. By learning how to interact differently with the environment, students will challenge the mainstream ideas and begin to question dominating ideologies about biodiversity and conservation, which may lead to action on their part.

Mining those Funds of Knowledge!

The teacher draws students' funds of knowledge through the "engage." The questions asked are geared to pre-assess students' previous knowledge and invite them to share about the practices they engage in. The teacher may choose to have students complete a K-W-L chart or concept map during this time. This will allow for students to write down their individual responses, which can be later shared through a Think-Pair-Share. At the start of the unit, the teacher could survey students about family practices and traditions such as hunting or fishing in preparation for some of the topics that will be covered.

Questions for Further Consideration

- How can teachers create a positive and culturally sensitive classroom for discussion of potentially sensitive topics?
- Are there cultural practices or traditions that should be included to make the lesson more relevant to students?

- How can teachers maximize the incorporation of students' experiences and prior knowledge into the lesson?

Notes

[1]The link to these resources can be found at http://tinyurl.com/Roman-Oliver-LP.

References

Ladson-Billings, G. (1995). But that's just good teaching! The case for culturally relevant pedagogy. *Theory Into Practice*, *34*(3), 159–165.

National Research Council. (2012). *A framework for K-12 science education: Practices, crosscutting concepts, and core ideas*. The National Academies Press. https://doi.org/10.17226/13165

NGSS Lead States. (2013). *Next Generation Science Standards: For states, by states*. The National Academies Press.

LESSON PLAN 5.2

Cultural Influences on Diet

Barbara J. Parks

Lesson Title

Cultural Influences on Diet

Grade Level/Course

Middle School-Health Science

Suggested Time

Two 90-minute blocks

Lesson Objectives

- Students will be able to compare and contrast the nutritional value of different food groups.
- Students will be able to identify factors that influence the dietary choices of different cultural groups.

Description

This lesson introduces students to the different nutritional groups through a collaborative activity. The goal is that students are able to identify factors that influence nutritional choices and the adoption of eating behaviors in different cultures.

Next Generation Science Standards

Crosscutting Concepts

- Cause and effect

Science and Engineering Practices

- Obtaining, evaluating, and communicating information

Disciplinary Core Ideas

"LS1.C: Organization for Matter and Energy Flow in Organisms—The sugar molecules thus formed contain carbon, hydrogen, and oxygen: their hydrocarbon backbones are used to make amino acids and other carbon-based molecules that can be assembled into larger molecules (such as proteins or DNA), used for example to form new cells." (National Research Council. 2012. *A Framework for K-12 Science Education: Practices, Crosscutting Concepts, and Core Ideas.* Washington, DC: The National Academies Press. https://doi.org/10.17226/13165, p. 147)

5E Lesson Plan

Day 1

Engage

The teacher will share the following: Growing up in the South (Georgia), my family enjoyed eating a lot of "soul food." What factors/things do you think influence our eating choices? Students will be asked and given one minute to think about this and then turn and talk with their elbow partner. Students will then be asked and encouraged to voluntarily share their responses to the whole group. The teacher will then ask students if they have foods/favorite dishes that are native to their cultures. Students will write this down and explain/compare their native/favorite food dish with the group members at their tables. The teacher will ask students to voluntarily share to the whole group, as well. The teacher will show students a brief video[1] on food and culture. The teacher will then explain that today's lesson will focus on identifying the ingredients and food groups that the ingredients belong to from their native/favorite dishes.

Explore

Students will work independently on the computer to research and write down the recipe/ingredients of their native/favorite dish. The class will be divided into groups, with five students in each group, representative of the five food groups. Each student in the group will represent one of the five food groups. Each student will take turns saying the ingredients that make up their native/favorite dish and they all will help each other determine what food group the ingredient belongs to. The group members (vegetables, fruits, dairy, grains, protein) will record the ingredients on their paper/list based on the group the ingredient belongs to. Students will also be asked to create a drawing or poster of their favorite dish labeling the ingredients and identifying the food groups that they belong to. Students will be asked the following:

- What recipe ingredients make up your native/favorite dish?

- What food groups do the ingredients of your native/favorite dish belong to?

Day 2

Explain

The teacher will ask students what they consider healthy food(s)/diets and how they determine that a food(s)/diet is healthy. The teacher will encourage and give students the opportunity to voluntarily share responses to the whole group. The teacher will lead students through a mini-lesson discussion and review websites on calories (i.e., Dietary Guidelines for Americans,[2] and MyPlate[3]). The teacher will then demonstrate the use of the Recipe Nutrition Calculator[4] website tool that students will be using.

Elaborate

Students will be asked to take out their family recipes that they verified with parents for the previous night's homework. Students will independently enter their native dish/favorite food recipe into the recipe nutrition calculator tool to determine the total calories of their native dish/meal/favorite food. Based on the total calorie counts, students will analyze the results and determine if they are within their recommended daily calorie intake range, using the Healthy Children[5] website. Students will rotate around the class comparing diets/total calorie counts from different cultures and groups to determine which ones are healthier. Students will be shown data about health conditions that are linked to our diet and asked to reflect on the following:

- Do you notice any differences in the prevalence of certain health conditions across the groups? Explain.
- What factors impact the prevalence of these health conditions in some groups?
- Reflect on today's activity. What are some ways in which we can be more intentional about eating healthier?

Evaluate

The teacher will be observing students and their responses throughout the lesson, checking for understanding. At the end of the lesson, students will complete a 3-2-1 summary on influences on food choices/eating behaviors and connect with one of the previous units on the food groups. Students' food groups artwork and visuals will be displayed on the student work wall to lead students into the next day's lesson. The teacher will be observing students and their responses throughout the lesson, checking for understanding. The teacher will ask students summarizing questions individually/whole group on what culture or group had the healthiest diet/native dish/favorite food. Also, students will be asked how they know the diet was the healthiest.

Culturally Relevant Practices

Academic Success

Students are engaged in inquiry. They are asked to identify ingredients from cultural recipes and classify them according to the different food groups. They research native recipes and use the ingredient information in the creation of posters or other visual creations of their choice of the different food groups. Students are then asked to consult parents on the validity of recipes, according to family and cultural traditions. By engaging students and their cultures, they tend to be more motivated and take accountability for their learning. The higher order inquiry and cultural exploration enriches the learning experiences for students.

Cultural Competence

Students bring in their background, cultural knowledge, and family practices in the learning experience and learning about other cultures/diets from around the world. This is observed throughout the different activities in the lesson. Students share their expertise in their cultural and lived experiences with their peers, while learning about others and their cultures as well. This exposure to the practices in other cultures helps develop appreciation and awareness, which are important in a culturally responsive learning environment.

Critical Consciousness

On Day 2, students will compare diets from different cultures/groups to see which ones are healthier. Students get to analyze the nutritional recommended daily calorie values and critically think to determine which native dish/diets are healthier. Students will be prompted to recognize how their nutritional choices are influenced by their upbringing and background. They are presented with data related to different health conditions that are linked to an individuals' dietary patterns. As they explore the data in relation to different groups (i.e. gender, ethnicity, socioeconomic status), they are asked to analyze and reflect on it. The goal is that students can pinpoint the link between cultural practices and certain health conditions. In doing this, the teacher aims to promote awareness around conditions that may be prevented by making healthier choices.

Mining those Funds of Knowledge!

Students are contributing their funds of knowledge into different lesson components. First, when they share about their favorite dishes during the "engage" and "explore" students are tapping into their knowledge and experiences with the different foods that are part of these dishes. As they share this with their classmates, they may recall its characteristics, ingredients, and modes of preparation. Some students may even cook these dishes and be able to contribute to the discussion with their expertise.

Questions for Further Consideration

- How could teachers emphasize the importance of healthy eating?
- How can teachers ensure that they are being sensitive to students that may have one of the health conditions explored?

Notes

[1] The link to this resource can be found at http://tinyurl.com/Roman-Oliver-LP.
[2] The link to this resource can be found at http://tinyurl.com/Roman-Oliver-LP.
[3] The link to this resource can be found at http://tinyurl.com/Roman-Oliver-LP.
[4] The link to this resource can be found at http://tinyurl.com/Roman-Oliver-LP.
[5] The link to this resource can be found at http://tinyurl.com/Roman-Oliver-LP.

References

Ladson-Billings, G. (1995). But that's just good teaching! The case for culturally relevant pedagogy. *Theory Into Practice*, *34*(3), 159–165.

National Research Council. (2012). *A Framework for K-12 science education: Practices, crosscutting concepts, and core ideas*. The National Academies Press. https://doi.org/10.17226/13165

NGSS Lead States. (2013). *Next Generation Science Standards: For states, by states*. The National Academies Press.

LESSON PLAN 5.3

Exploring Mendelian Inheritance Patterns

Anne Norviel

Lesson Title

Exploring Mendelian Inheritance Patterns

Grade Level/Course

High School-Biology

Suggested Time

Two 90-minute blocks

Learning Objectives

- Students will be able to describe Mendelian inheritance patterns.
- Students will model genetic crosses to demonstrate how traits are inherited.

Description

This lesson introduces students to Gregor Mendel as well as his genetic discoveries. The lesson anticipates that students have vaguely been introduced to the concept of Mendelian inheritance patterns. Through the lesson, students acquire the key vocabulary needed to understand genetics and inheritance patterns. They will practice using Punnett squares and identifying the outcome of genetic crosses. In addition, students model how genetic inheritance occurs.

Next Generation Science Standards

Crosscutting Concepts

- Systems and system models
- Structure and function

Science and Engineering Practices

- Obtaining, evaluating, and communicating information
- Developing and using models

Disciplinary Core Ideas

"LS3.A: Inheritance of Traits—Each chromosome consists of a single very long DNA molecule, and each gene on the chromosome is a particular segment of that DNA. The instructions for forming species' characteristics are carried in DNA. All cells in an organism have the same genetic content, but the genes used (expressed) by the cell may be regulated in different ways. Not all DNA codes for a protein; some segments of DNA are involved in regulatory or structural functions, and some have no as-yet known function." (National Research Council. 2012. *A Framework for K-12 Science Education: Practices, Crosscutting Concepts, and Core Ideas*. Washington, DC: The National Academies Press. https://doi.org/10.17226/13165, p. 158)

5E Lesson

Day 1

Engage

To begin, the teacher will discuss how we all have different and similar traits. The teacher will pass out the worksheet, An *Inventory of My Traits*. Before the students begin, the teacher will ask them to add a column to the far right where they will write who they received the trait from or someone who has a similar trait (this is to be sensitive as some students may not know their biological parents' traits). The teacher will provide an example by finding a couple of students who share a similar trait as the teacher. As students work through the chart, the teacher will show images for clarification using Observable Human Characteristics.[1] After students have completed the chart, the teacher will lead a class discussion prompting students to hypothesize which traits are dominant or recessive. In other words, students will identify which traits have a greater or lesser chance of being passed down to the next generation. The teacher will ask students to add an "R" or "D" next to each trait. At this time, the teacher will encourage students to share why they think this is the case. This would prompt students to talk about how the trait is observed in other members of the family.

Explore

Students will select one of the traits they have identified as prominent in their family to research further. After students have selected a trait, they may be placed in pairs or small groups. They will investigate the frequency of the trait in different parts of the world. The teacher may encourage students to explore the implications of this trait for different cultures as well (including theirs). For example, a darker skin tone is the result of higher levels of melanin in the skin. This can protect against the UV waves produced by the sun, which could cause mutations and increase the risk of skin cancer. Students will create infographics, posters, or slides to present this information to the class.

Day 2

Explain

Prior to students entering the room, the teacher will create a chart on the board with four columns and seven rows. The first column will be titled *key words* and include the following vocabulary terms: allele, dominant, recessive, phenotype, genotype, homozygous, and heterozygous. The subsequent columns will be titled *definition*, *example*, and *not an example*. The teacher will ask students to replicate the chart in their notes. Next, students will read and annotate 12.3A: Mendel's Laws of Heredity.[2] As they read, they can complete the vocabulary chart in their notes. During a class discussion, the teacher will go over the chart adding the correct answers to the board. Next, the teacher will show an image of an attached vs. unattached earlobe. The teacher will ask the following questions: If we use the letter E to represent attached earlobes, what is the genotype for a heterozygous individual? What is the individual's phenotype? If we use the letter e for unattached earlobes, what is the individual's genotype? What are all of the possible genotypes for attached earlobes? After the discussion of the correct answers, the teacher will ask students to pick one trait each from their *Inventory of Traits* worksheet to practice Punnett squares. As the students work, the teacher will walk through the room offering guidance and checking for correct answers. If the answers are incorrect, the teacher will help the students.

Elaborate

During this time, the teacher will explain both monohybrid crosses and homologous chromosomes and why they are important. Then, students will use pipe cleaners to create homologous chromosome models for one of the dominant traits on their worksheets. Preferably, the student would pick a trait they have not worked with previously. After they create the chromosomes, the teacher will lead students to create a Punnett square in their notes or the teacher could print Punnett squares. Students will use the Punnett square and the homologous chromosome models to show the possible allele combinations of their traits. The two sets of chromosomes now represent the mother and father chromosomes. Next, students will do the same with a second Punnett square and a set of recessive alleles. The recessive alleles should be a different color pipe cleaner than the dominant alleles. Each time students complete the Punnett squares they will pull the combinations into the appropriate box and then write the allele combination. This allows students to be tactile and realize that alleles really do exist. They are not just letters.

Days 1 & 2

Evaluate

There is pre-assessment of students' ideas during the "engage." As students share their hypothesis about which traits may be dominant or recessive, the teacher should ask for them to explain their answer. Their responses may reveal some preconceptions about the strength of certain genetic traits. During the "explore," students' research skills are also evaluated. The teacher should assess how well students were able to answer the guiding questions for the task. During the "explain," the teacher also assesses students' comprehension of the concepts of genotype and phenotype. Finally, at the last stage, students will complete the Mendelian Inheritance Patterns Analysis Questions[3] to check for comprehension. The teacher will lead a class discussion to go over the answers.

Culturally Relevant Practices

Academic Success

Two NGSS aspects are directly aligned to the activities within this lesson. Students are creating models to demonstrate the inheritance of traits. Students are also asked to describe their observations using the resource provided. As students conduct research during the "explore," they are tasked with locating resources that are reliable and practice data analysis/interpretation skills as well. Evaluating the validity and reliability of a resource is an important aspect of scientific literacy.

Cultural Competence

Students use their background knowledge during the "engage" as they identify physical traits in their family. They use this knowledge to hypothesize if a trait is easier to be passed on compared to another. For instance, they may recall family members that have the trait versus others who do not and use this information to draw conclusions. However, the teacher should be intentional about guiding students towards understanding that the frequency of a trait in a population does not necessarily determine its strength or probability of being inherited. Students also have a chance to discuss how the prominence of certain traits may be beneficial for specific groups of people, based on their location or other factors. In doing this, students can reflect on how the genetic traits they possess are important or useful.

Critical Consciousness

Although not featured in this lesson, as a follow up teachers may assign students to watch the movie *Gattaca*. The movie is based on the idea that parents will be able to select certain genetic traits for their children. The teacher could ask students to reflect on the following prompts and discuss these the next day during the opening of the lesson:

- What are the implications of being able to select an individual's traits before they are born?
- Would it be a good idea if potential employers were able to conduct DNA tests to find out our abilities as related to a job? Why or why not?

These questions give students an opportunity to reflect on the potential implications of biotechnology as related to ethics and social justice.

Mining those Funds of Knowledge!

Students' funds of knowledge are brought into the lesson through the "engage." As students share their ideas about the different traits and their perceived dominance, they are utilizing their past experiences and hypothesizing. Students' selection of a trait during the "explore" is driven by their interest and curiosity as well. Throughout this stage, students use their understanding of the trait to evaluate its prevalence and importance for certain groups.

Questions for Further Consideration

- What other factors should teachers take into consideration when selecting the traits for students to analyze?
- What additional assistance or guidance do students need to conduct the research?

Notes

[1]The link to this resource can be found at http://tinyurl.com/Roman-Oliver-LP.
[2]The link to this resource can be found at http://tinyurl.com/Roman-Oliver-LP.
[3]The link to this resource can be found at http://tinyurl.com/Roman-Oliver-LP.

References

College Board. (2021). *Pre-AP biology teacher resources* (Units 3 and 4 ed.). College Board.

Ladson-Billings, G. (1995). But that's just good teaching! The case for culturally relevant pedagogy. *Theory Into Practice*, *34*(3), 159–165.

National Research Council. (2012). *A framework for K-12 science education: Practices, crosscutting concepts, and core ideas*. The National Academies Press. https://doi.org/10.17226/13165

NGSS Lead States. (2013). *Next Generation Science Standards: For states, by states*. The National Academies Press.

LESSON PLAN 5.4

Diversity Benefits Us All

Melissa Volante

Lesson Title
Diversity Benefits Us All

Grade Level/Course
High School-Biology

Suggested Time
Three 90-minute blocks

Learning Objectives

- Students will compare and contrast the main characteristics of each earth biome.
- Students will explain the importance of biodiversity in ecosystems.

Description
This lesson plan introduces students to the different earth biomes. Students have an opportunity to work collaboratively to explore different biomes and identify their characteristics (e.g., fauna, flora, temperature, etc.). Additionally, students are guided towards acknowledging the importance of diversity in the human population. This is done by recognizing the importance of biodiversity in the natural world, through a discussion of the benefits that this brings to all.

Next Generation Science Standards

Crosscutting Concepts

- Patterns
- Stability and change

Science and Engineering Practices

- Obtaining, evaluating, and communicating information

Disciplinary Core Ideas

"LS4.D: Biodiversity and Humans—Biodiversity is increased by the formation of new species (speciation) and decreased by the loss of species (extinction). Humans depend on the living world for the resources and other benefits provided by biodiversity. But human activity is also having adverse impacts on biodiversity through overpopulation, overexploitation, habitat destruction, pollution, introduction of invasive species, and climate change. Thus sustaining biodiversity so that ecosystem functioning and productivity are maintained is essential to supporting and enhancing life on Earth. Sustaining biodiversity also aids humanity by preserving landscapes of recreational or inspirational value." (National Research Council. 2012. *A Framework for K-12 Science Education: Practices, Crosscutting Concepts, and Core Ideas*. Washington, DC: The National Academies Press. https://doi.org/10.17226/13165, p. 166)

5E Lesson

Day 1

Engage

The teacher will instruct students to find someone in the room who has grown up in a different area than them or whose parents or grandparents are from a different country than their parents or grandparents. The students will ask each other the following questions:

- What are some plants that grow in your area?
- What are some animals that you are familiar with in your area?

Students will record their partner's answers in a t-chart (e.g., animals and plants).

Students will volunteer to share out some of the answers from the opening activity and the teacher will record them on the board. Then the teacher will explain that their homework for the evening is to go home and ask (call if needed) their grandparents or other relatives in their family the same questions they asked their partner and record the answers. After this discussion, the teacher will talk about how it is good and enriching for us to learn about others' lives, cultures, and families. We all have differences and similarities, and that is what makes the world work and what makes life fun and interesting. Learning about other cultures also makes us more well-rounded, challenges our current thinking, and helps us to see life through someone else's eyes. Just like in the different biomes of the world, the species there have adapted to the climate they are in, so we often adapt based on the situations or experiences we have or the places we come from.

Explore

The students will work in pairs to complete a card sort[1] (pages 3–6 of the resource). For this activity, students will be provided cards with pictures of different animals and plants. They will have poster boards throughout the room labeled with the name of each biome. The students will work in pairs and rotate through the room. They will read a brief description on each poster that describes the temperature, elevation, rainfall, and other general characteristics of the biome. Pairs of students will place the cards in the biomes where they believe the different species of plants and animals belong. Students will be collaborating and using their background knowledge to make these decisions.

Explain

After each pair has visited each biome and placed their cards, the teacher will go over each poster and identify the species that have been placed. The teacher will ask the class to agree or disagree with the placement of the cards. From here, a discussion may initiate about the needs of plants and animals based on their environment. A video[2] will be played introducing students to each of the different types of biomes and giving a brief physical description of each. After the video, the teacher will ask the class the following questions:

- What factors impact the characteristics of a biome?
- What could you say about the biodiversity in these?

Day 2

Explain (continued)

The teacher will introduce the Biome Vacation Video Project. Students will be working in groups to create an entertaining social media video (i.e., TikTok,

Instagram, etc.) that features an assigned biome and its characteristics as well as showcases things that families could do while on vacation there.

Elaborate

During this time, the teacher will create groups and assign a different biome to each. The purpose of this task is to explore further the characteristics of the biomes. The students will research the following areas before making the video:

- Locations of biome around the world
- Average inches of yearly precipitation
- Average temperature range
- Three plants in the biome
- Three animals in the biome
- Three activities that a person on vacation could do in the biome
- Three things you would need to pack for a trip to the biome

The teacher will be walking around during this time to answer questions, help with problem areas, and provide individual or group feedback on the research being recorded. Groups will begin creating settings if needed, creating slides, and arranging information to record their videos.

Day 3

Elaborate (continued)

Students will present their videos and the class will create a summarizing chart with the general characteristics of each biome (i.e., temperature, precipitation, latitude, longitude, animals, and plants). The teacher will guide students in reflecting on the biodiversity in these areas. Students will access the United Nations' Biodiversity Explained: Facts, Myths and the Race to Protect It[3] resource. Working in pairs, students will read the article and highlight anything that stands out to them. The teacher will lead a discussion on the importance of biodiversity by asking students to share one thing that they learned from the reading. The teacher will then ask students to consider the diversity in the classroom, school, city, and country. The teacher will ask students the following questions:

- Consider the diversity in humans as a population. In what ways has this changed lately?

- Now that you know a bit more about the importance of biodiversity in nature, why do you think diversity in the human population is important?
- You explored some threats to biodiversity; what are some threats to diversity in humans as a population? What is one thing you would change, if you could? Why?

Students will be encouraged to discuss these ideas and write their thoughts in their journals at this time.

Days 1 & 2

Evaluate
Students' previous knowledge about biomes is pre-assessed during the "engage." As students share about the areas in which they live and activities they engage in, the teacher may guide students with questions to provide additional details or compare/contrast their regions. During the "explore," students' ideas about different species and where they belong is observed as they place the pictures on the posters. As students research the different biomes and create their videos, the teacher may ask questions that guide students' understanding of how different factors impact the biodiversity in these areas. Students present their videos, giving the teacher an opportunity to evaluate their understanding of biomes. Finally, students' ideas about diversity in general can be assessed through the informal discussion and their reflective journal writing.

Culturally Relevant Practices

Academic Success

During the "elaborate," students work collaboratively to obtain information about each biome. This information will need to be evaluated based on the validity of the source and then communicated through a nontraditional method (social media video). This aligns with the NGSS (2013) scientific practice of "Obtaining, evaluating, and communicating information" (p. 8). Students also apply digital skills in the creation of the video. The reflective nature of the final task allows the teacher to tap into higher cognitive skills such as synthesis and connection (Wisconsin Center for Education Products and Services, 2023).

Cultural Competence

This lesson involves students working in groups. These groups will be a mix of grade averages, cultural backgrounds, and personalities. Allowing the students to share with the class what they may have learned from their relatives about their cultures or traditions allows them to incorporate their heritage and experiences. This reminds them that their experiences matter to our class as a whole, and we can all learn new things and celebrate those differences. This will help students feel more confident and valued which in turn helps them learn and grow. In addition to the exposure to different ideas through the collaborative activity, students work on creating a social media video using a popular platform. Many students love watching these videos and sharing them with their friends or family. Therefore, this is an important aspect of their youth cultural practices. By allowing students to create their own videos and share these with the class, we are allowing them to utilize some of their creative skills.

Critical Consciousness

Students exercise critical consciousness through the last discussion and reflective writing exercise. When students are asked to connect the concept of biodiversity (and its threats) to human population diversity, they are guided to consider ways in which we have historically responded to change in this area. Furthermore, they are asked to think of ways in which we could move towards integration of different cultures. In doing this, students that have moved from different cities, states, or countries can draw from their experiences and discuss areas of improvement.

Mining those Funds of Knowledge!

Students have an opportunity to share about the characteristics of regions/areas that they are familiar with. In this way, their expertise in this area is utilized as a way to start the lesson. Whether they see these as concepts related to science or not, their context and surroundings have been a part of their upbringing and experience. For instance, if students have been raised in rural communities in which farms of pastures are common, they may have knowledge about temperature and soil conditions. Additionally, if students come from a different country, they are able to share some of the characteristics of their home town that may be unique and different from those nearby. Students also are able to utilize their creative skills related to video recording and editing. As mentioned in the previous section, social media videos have become very popular among middle and high school students. Some students identify themselves as "influencers" if they have a large following, for instance. The "elaborate" activity in this lesson allows them to use these funds of knowledge for the purpose of sharing their learning in the science classroom.

Questions for Further Consideration

- What are the technology requirements for this lesson? How can teachers plan for this in advance to minimize disruption to the learning process?
- How could teachers show sensitivity towards immigrant students who may be experiencing challenges?

Notes

[1]The link to this resource can be found at http://tinyurl.com/Roman-Oliver-LP.
[2]The link to this resource can be found at http://tinyurl.com/Roman-Oliver-LP.
[3]The link to this resource can be found at http://tinyurl.com/Roman-Oliver-LP.

References

Ladson-Billings, G. (1995). But that's just good teaching! The case for culturally relevant pedagogy. *Theory Into Practice*, *34*(3), 159–165.

National Research Council. (2012). *A framework for K-12 science education: Practices, crosscutting concepts, and core ideas*. The National Academies Press. https://doi.org/10.17226/13165

NGSS Lead States. (2013). *Next Generation Science Standards: For states, by states*. The National Academies Press.

LESSON PLAN 5.5

Rhymes and Rhythms of the Body

Ansley Talafous

Lesson Title
Rhymes and Rhythms of the Body

Grade Level/Course
Middle School-Life Science

Suggested Time
Two 90-minute blocks

Learning Objectives

- Identify and describe the major human body systems, including their structures and functions.
- Explain the components and functions of a specific human body system.

Description
This lesson introduces students to the interactions in the systems of the body using scenarios. Students will discuss how different body systems interact and collaborate to create a rap song to perform in class.

Next Generation Science Standards

Crosscutting Concepts

- Structure and function
- Cause and effect
- Systems and system models

Science and Engineering Practices

- Obtaining, evaluating, and communicating information
- Constructing explanations

Disciplinary Core Ideas
"LS1.A: Structure and Function—In multicellular organisms, the body is a system of multiple interacting subsystems. These subsystems are groups of cells that work together to form tissues and organs that are specialized for particular

body functions." (National Research Council. 2012. *A Framework for K-12 Science Education: Practices, Crosscutting Concepts, and Core Ideas*. Washington, DC: The National Academies Press. https://doi.org/10.17226/13165, p. 143)

5E Lesson

Day 1

Engage

To capture the students' attention and pique their curiosity, the teacher will start the lesson with a picture/clip from a popular medical TV show like *Grey's Anatomy* or a documentary that highlights medical professionals discussing the complexities of the human body and its systems and begin with a brief discussion about *Grey's Anatomy* and its popularity. Ask students:

- What did you find interesting or surprising about the interactions between different body systems in the video?
- Can you think of any real-world situations where knowledge of body system interactions is essential?

Explore

Divide students into small groups. Distribute scenario[1] cards to each group, each containing a different body system interaction scenario. In their groups, students discuss and develop solutions to their scenarios, applying what they learned from the clips.

Explain

Each group prepares a brief presentation to share their scenario and solution with the class. As each group presents, the rest of the class takes notes or writes down questions to ask after the presentations.

Day 2

Elaborate

Show students the following video[2] of a song about the human body. Ask students to notice and take notes of the systems featured, interactions, the lyrics, or type of music/rhythms featured. Explain to students that one of the goals for today is to create a rap song of an interaction between two systems of the body. Divide students into small groups of their choice and assign each group a specific body system interaction to focus on. Provide resources,[3] such as diagrams and textbooks, to help students research and understand the interactions. Guide students in brainstorming and drafting lyrics for their rap or song. In small groups, have students work collaboratively to create their raps or songs and decide on lyrics, rhythm, and melody. Encourage creativity and exploration of musical elements (e.g., rhyme, metaphor) to enhance the song's impact. At the end of the lesson, each group performs their rap or song to the class, explaining the body system interactions they have depicted. The rest of the class will score the performance using the following rubric.[4] After each presentation, ask the class to describe the interactions presented in the song.

Days 1 & 2

Evaluate

Students' ideas are pre-assessed through the "explore/explain" activity as they use problem-solving skills to determine what is causing the symptoms in each scenario. Their understanding about the interactions between different body systems is also evaluated when they create lyrics that represent these.

Culturally Relevant Practices

Academic Success

In this lesson, students use problem-solving skills to identify possible issues within the scenarios. This allows them to explain the causes and effects of different conditions related to different body systems. Additionally, as they conduct the research for the interactions in their respective body systems, they "obtain and evaluate" the information from the different resources and "communicate" their learning through the song performance.

Cultural Competence

Using a popular TV show during the "engage" allows for connections with youth culture. If the teacher finds out that a show other than *Grey's Anatomy* is more popular among the students, a different clip may be used. Online TV streaming has become the norm in the last few years and many students enjoy finding new shows to binge watch. Connecting the concepts in the lesson with a popular show allows for teachers to bring some of the students' home practices into the classroom. Most importantly, when students engage in the writing and performance of the song, different skill sets are incorporated. Many students are into rap music and other popular kinds of rhythms. The teacher may adapt this activity and have students create any type of song, not just rap. This connection with youth culture is important as music is a significant part of their everyday lives. Some students write and produce music as a hobby as well. Many also sing or play different instruments both in and out of school.

Critical Consciousness

Acknowledging the students' cultural backgrounds and preferences, the lesson cleverly incorporates popular culture, such as the TV show *Grey's Anatomy*, creating a bridge between classroom content and pop culture. Students are also encouraged to use critical thinking as they evaluate the different scenarios during the "explore." Most importantly, students discuss their ideas and are exposed to alternative points of view before making predictions. The adaptation of the music activity to encompass various genres beyond rap exemplifies a commitment to recognizing and embracing the diverse cultural experiences and preferences of the students.

Mining those Funds of Knowledge!

The knowledge that students have about the systems of the body, learned through TV shows, can also be tapped into during the "engage" and "explore." A good reminder for teachers is that students are exposed to a lot of science concepts through media. As teachers, we can incorporate this informal knowledge acquired, but also guide students into being critical about it. As mentioned in the cultural competence section, students use their music skills during the "elaborate" as they create and eventually perform their song lyrics. Some students are skilled in writing lyrics, singing, or even using music mixing software or playing an instrument. All these skills can be showcased during this time. When the teacher adopts a role of facilitator and allows students to create freely, they are able to use the different funds of knowledge they bring into the classroom and showcase these. This also exposes other students to different music styles.

Questions for Further Consideration

- How can teachers accommodate different learning styles and preferences in the creation of the song?
- Are there alternative ways for students to express their understanding beyond song lyrics?
- How can teachers create a supportive environment that allows students to freely express their creativity during the song creation activity?
- Are there any potential cultural biases in the materials or examples used, and how can teachers address or mitigate them?

Notes

[1] The link to this resource can be found at http://tinyurl.com/Roman-Oliver-LP.
[2] The link to this resource can be found at http://tinyurl.com/Roman-Oliver-LP.
[3] The link to this resource can be found at http://tinyurl.com/Roman-Oliver-LP.
[4] The link to this resource can be found at http://tinyurl.com/Roman-Oliver-LP.

References

Ladson-Billings, G. (1995). But that's just good teaching! The case for culturally relevant pedagogy. *Theory Into Practice, 34*(3), 159–165.

National Research Council. (2012). *A framework for K-12 science education: Practices, crosscutting concepts, and core ideas*. The National Academies Press. https://doi.org/10.17226/1316

NGSS Lead States. (2013). *Next Generation Science Standards: For states, by states*. The National Academies Press.

LESSON PLAN 5.6

How Do Fireworks Work?

Larry Layfield

Lesson Title

How Do Fireworks Work?

Grade Level/Course

High School-Chemistry

Suggested Time

Two 90-minute blocks

Learning Objectives

- Students will be able to identify substances using a flame test.
- Students will be able to discuss cultural elements related to the use of fireworks.

Description

The purpose of this lesson is to provide students with an opportunity to identify an unknown substance based on its flame test colors. This opens the doors to much deeper conversations about chemical properties and describing atoms. The flame test lab is used as a visual representation of a much larger concept. Additionally, students explore the significance of fireworks in other cultures and their celebrations.

Next Generation Science Standards

Crosscutting Concepts

- Patterns
- Energy and matter

Science and Engineering Practices

- Analyzing and interpreting data
- Obtaining, evaluating, and communicating information

Disciplinary Core Ideas

"PS1.A: Structure and Properties of Matter—Each pure substance has characteristic physical and chemical properties (for any bulk quantity under given conditions) that can be used to identify it." (National Research Council. 2012. *A Framework for K-12 Science Education: Practices, Crosscutting Concepts, and Core Ideas*. Washington, DC: The National Academies Press. https://doi.org/10.17226/13165, p. 108)

5E Lesson

Day 1

Engage

The teacher will post a picture of fireworks on the board and provide students with a sticky note. The students will record what they know about fireworks, and try to answer the question: "Why do fireworks produce multiple colors?" using their previous knowledge. Students will contribute their answers to a large Post-It paper in the front of the classroom. Then, the teacher will show a video[1] about fireworks and ask students to turn and talk with their table partner to share new information presented in the video. After students have had the opportunity to discuss among themselves, the teacher will hold a class discussion to allow table groups to share what they remember about fireworks and the activated prior knowledge the picture or video shared. The teacher will create a list of common themes and observations.

Explore

Before beginning the lab, the teacher will ask students to think about ways that scientists identify materials they might be unfamiliar with. The purpose of starting this conversation is to provide students with the opportunity to activate their prior knowledge. The teacher will create a list on the board with some of these techniques. The technique introduced in the lab experiment is used as a way to identify elements or compounds. The students will explore the phenomenon through the flame test lab.[2] The students work in groups to test different known and unknown solutions and record their observations based on the flame color change.

Day 2

Explain

The teacher will conduct a mini-lesson explaining the science behind the flame test lab and why the test is used to help identify elements and compounds. During the mini-lesson, the teacher will provide students with guided instruction on the process of energy absorption and photon emission.

Elaborate

Students will read an article[3] that explains how fireworks are used around the world in different cultural settings. The teacher will assign groups of students a different part of the world to explore further. The students will investigate how fireworks are used to celebrate different holidays or events in the respective countries. Then, students will share about how fireworks are an important part of celebrations in this part of the world.

Days 1 & 2

Evaluate

Evaluation occurs at different stages of the 5E cycle. For example, pre-assessment occurs during the "engage" as students share their experiences and ideas about fireworks. During the "explore," students are asked several analysis questions at the end of the laboratory activity. This is tied to the scientific practice of analyzing and interpreting data. Students are also asked to investigate the use of fireworks in different cultures and share their findings during the "elaborate." This allows teachers to assess their ability to obtain and communicate information.

Culturally Relevant Practices

Academic Success

Students are engaged in a structured inquiry through the laboratory activity. Working in groups, they have the opportunity to conduct a test on different substances to identify the elements or compounds present. After testing different known substances, students then determine the color of two unknown solutions. Further, students are then asked to reflect on two questions about what color different solutions might make. This comes from students' understanding that the metal ions cause the color to change—which is not provided in the background or procedure. In other words, students are being asked to make predictions.

Cultural Competence

This lesson allows students to engage in, explore, and elaborate on their knowledge of fireworks. In most students' lives they have seen fireworks as a celebratory event and visual pleasure. In my personal life, before taking a chemistry course, I always wanted to learn how fireworks were operated and what made the different colors. Fireworks were significant for me and my family growing up because they provided the opportunity for the family to get together and enjoy the weather while watching them. The fireworks served as another means of the family spending quality time with one another, whether they were for the Fourth of July or New Year's Day. The goal with this lesson is to bring students' culture into the classroom by providing them the space to learn more about the emission of a photon, which creates the colorful lights we see in the sky. The "elaborate" portion of the lesson sequence provides students with the opportunity to find out how fireworks are used in different parts of the world, exposing them to important elements of culture that they may be unfamiliar with.

Critical Consciousness

Although not featured in this lesson, for homework, students may be assigned to read the article "Crowd-Pleasing Fireworks Are Not So Pleasing to the Planet."[4] While some of the activities in class focused on the cultural importance of fireworks, the article explores how the use of fireworks may impact the environment. Students will reflect on the areas that are negatively affected by the use of fireworks and come prepared the next day to discuss if the more eco-friendly alternatives would be a good option in the United States.

Mining those Funds of Knowledge!

Students' funds of knowledge are brought into the lesson at different points. First, students are asked to share their knowledge and experience with fireworks during the "engage." During the "explore" they also contribute to the discussion by sharing examples of how scientists investigate or find out more about substances they encounter in nature.

Questions for Further Consideration

- How can teachers increase the level of inquiry during the laboratory activity?
- What are some safety precautions that teachers should take into consideration when preparing for this lesson?
- What are some grouping strategies that teachers should consider, for both the laboratory and the "elaborate" stage?

Notes

[1]The link to this resource can be found at http://tinyurl.com/Roman-Oliver-LP.
[2]The link to this resource can be found at http://tinyurl.com/Roman-Oliver-LP.
[3]The link to this resource can be found at http://tinyurl.com/Roman-Oliver-LP.
[4]The link to this resource can be found at http://tinyurl.com/Roman-Oliver-LP.

References

Ladson-Billings, G. (1995). But that's just good teaching! The case for culturally relevant pedagogy. *Theory Into Practice*, *34*(3), 159–165.

National Research Council. (2012). *A framework for K-12 science education: Practices, crosscutting concepts, and core ideas*. The National Academies Press. https://doi.org/10.17226/13165

NGSS Lead States. (2013). *Next Generation Science Standards: For states, by states*. The National Academies Press.

LESSON PLAN 5.7

Energy Transformations

Sarah Brown

Lesson Title
Energy Transformations

Grade Level/Course
Middle School-Physical Sciences

Suggested Time
Two 90-minute blocks

Learning Objective

- Students will be able to describe the relationships between kinetic energy, mass, speed, potential energy, mass, and height in objects.

Description
In this lesson, students are introduced to the concepts of kinetic and potential energy using different scenarios. Students collaborate to discuss the transformations of energy and share what they learned with the class. Then, students use an interactive simulation to explore the energy changes that occur when skateboarding.

Next Generation Science Standards

Crosscutting Concept

- Energy and matter

Science and Engineering Practices

- Constructing explanations and designing solutions
- Analyzing and interpreting data

Disciplinary Core Idea
"PS3-B: Mathematical expressions, which quantify how the stored energy in a system depends on its configuration (e.g., relative positions of charged particles, compression of a spring) and how kinetic energy depends on mass and

speed, allow the concept of conservation of energy to be used to predict and describe system behavior. The availability of energy limits what can occur in any system" (National Research Council. 2012. *A Framework for K-12 Science Education: Practices, Crosscutting Concepts, and Core Ideas.* Washington, DC: The National Academies Press. https://doi.org/10.17226/13165, p. 126)

5E Lesson

Day 1

Engage

The teacher will ask students to brainstorm examples of energy around them using a bubble map. They will also write down what they know about energy in general. Using these examples and ideas, students will pair up with a classmate to come up with a definition of energy. The teacher will ask each pair to voluntarily share one idea and one example. The teacher will use these to create a formal definition of energy and write it on the board.

Explore

Students will work in small groups to complete a station activity.[1] Each station will feature a different scenario in which energy is being transformed. Students will read each scenario and review the picture that is featured. Students will identify the types of energy involved in the scenario as well as the transformation. A list of different types of energy and their definition will be provided.

Day 2

Explain

The teacher will ask one student from each group to select one of the scenarios to share their answers with the class. The teacher will add to their explanation or make corrections as needed.

Elaborate

The teacher will get students' attention using a short video clip showcasing professional skateboarders performing impressive tricks and stunts. The physics behind each trick will be explained briefly. The teacher will say: "Just like professional skateboarders master the physics of their sport, we're going to explore how motion, force, and energy work together to create those amazing moves." The teacher will connect this directly to the students' experiences and interests, emphasizing that they will not just be learning physics but applying it to a real-world, exciting context. The students will be directed to a PhET interactive simulation,[2] allowing them to explore skateboarding scenarios and manipulate variables in real time. The teacher will provide clear instructions and a brief tutorial for using the simulation. Students will work individually or in pairs to explore specific skateboarding scenarios within the simulation and answer a series of related questions.

Days 1 & 2

Evaluate
Students' understanding of concepts is evaluated through the "engage," which acts as a pre-assessment. Students' misconceptions are also identified at this point. As they share their findings from the different scenarios, the teacher evaluates their understanding of the different types of energy and provides feedback. Finally, as students answer the questions during the "elaborate," the teacher can see how they have transferred these ideas to a new scenario/context.

Culturally Relevant Practices

Academic Success
When students share their answers and engage in discussion with their classmates, they compare and contrast some of their ideas about energy. Students apply their knowledge of the different types of energy through the scenarios presented in the stations, as well as the simulation. Both comparing and contrasting and application are higher-order thinking skills that are aligned with scientific practices as well.

Cultural Competence
Many students either practice skateboarding or another type of extreme sport. While they may not be thinking about energy when engaged in these, the teacher will be intentional about making these connections throughout the lesson. Sports, in general, are an important part of youth culture, and engagement in sport-related activities takes a significant portion of time after school.

Mining those Funds of Knowledge!

Students contribute their knowledge and skills about skateboarding or other examples of similar activities both during the "engage" and the "elaborate." Students' experiences are drawn by the teacher through the use of questions and discussion of energy transformations. The teacher may survey students at the start of the unit to find out which other extreme sports students participate in. The scenarios and simulations used should be tailored to these to give students an opportunity to contribute with their expertise. Demonstrations may even be encouraged if there is adequate space for it. Safety measures need to be in place, however.

Questions for Further Consideration

- What previous knowledge is important for students to have before engaging in the "explore"?
- What are the technology requirements of the "elaborate"?
- How can teachers ensure that the lesson is accessible for all learners?

Notes

[1]The link to this resource can be found at http://tinyurl.com/Roman-Oliver-LP.
[2]The link to this resource can be found at http://tinyurl.com/Roman-Oliver-LP.

References

Ladson-Billings, G. (1995). But that's just good teaching! The case for culturally relevant pedagogy. *Theory Into Practice*, *34*(3), 159–165.

National Research Council. (2012). *A framework for K-12 science education: Practices, crosscutting concepts, and core ideas*. The National Academies Press. https://doi.org/10.17226/13165

NGSS Lead States. (2013). *Next Generation Science Standards: For states, by states*. The National Academies Press.

LESSON PLAN 5.8

Heat Transfer in the Kitchen

Perri Lennon

Lesson Title

Heat Transfer in the Kitchen

Grade Level/Course

Middle School-Physical Sciences

Suggested Time

Two 90-minute blocks

Learning Objectives

- Students will be able to investigate and display the effects of heat transfer on molecular motion as it relates to culinary recipes.

Description

This lesson introduces students to the different types of heat transfer. Students collaborate to create posters that illustrate some of their favorite dishes and how conduction, convection, and radiation are used as modes of preparation.

Next Generation Science Standards

Crosscutting Concepts

- Energy and matter
- Systems and system models

Science and Engineering Practices

- Construct explanations
- Developing and using models

Disciplinary Core Ideas

"PS3.B: Conservation of Energy and Energy Transfer—The amount of energy transfer needed to change the temperature of a matter sample by a given amount depends on the nature of the matter, the size of the sample, and the environment." (National Research Council. 2012. *A Framework for K-12 Science*

Education: Practices, Crosscutting Concepts, and Core Ideas. Washington, DC: The National Academies Press. https://doi.org/10.17226/13165, p. 126)

5E Lesson

Day 1

Engage
The teacher will show a short clip[1] of different types of foods cooking. The teacher will ask: "How do we use heat in different ways for cooking?" Students will write their responses in their interactive notebooks.

Explore
The teacher will instruct students to select a "staple" dish that represents their ethnicity or nationality. The dish could be a savory or sweet one. Using the internet[2] or a cookbook, students will find step-by-step cooking directions for the food to use as a resource throughout this activity. A blank sheet of paper will be used to "pre-plan" the poster; on their scrap papers, students will jot down the information that will be written on the final poster and sketch drawings. Once students have finished collecting their information, they must seek teacher approval to receive their final poster board. Everything recorded on the scrap paper should be transferred to the larger poster board. The remainder of time allotted for this activity in class should be used to add color, sketch, and organize the board. The following sections need to be included in their posters:

- Name of the meal
- Definition of the three types of heat transfer—conduction, convection, and radiation. Although some recipes do not require all three, it is important that students are familiar with each.
- Description of the main heat transfer used in the recipe (a three-sentence explanation of why it is the main type of heat transfer should be included). As students read through the recipe, they must identify at least three steps that clearly include a form of heat transfer. For example, "Step one: Roasting your marshmallows over the fire is a form of radiation." Each step should include a small drawing—if the example were used, it would include a drawing of a fire. All three steps should be noted on the scratch paper.

- A drawing of the dish containing arrows to identify the flow of the thermal energy and molecular motion. Finally, the poster will include a drawing of the food. It is required that this drawing contain arrows to display the flow of thermal energy. Ideally, the drawing will show what the heat source is—grill, pan, pot, etc.—and how heat travels between the food and the original source of heat.
- In another section, students should include a statement of a couple of sentences to explain why the dish is relevant to their culture.

Day 2

Explain

Students will present their poster to their elbow partners and discuss what similarities and differences exist between their recipes and heat transfer methods. For the presentations, students may be asked to bring in their dish to share with the class—if available to do so. While bringing in the food physically is not a requirement, all students must share their poster boards and submit their scrap paper for full credit. The teacher will have students share with the class voluntarily at least one example of each type of heat transfer. The teacher will ask questions to check on students' understanding.

Elaborate

To extend their learning further, students are asked to consider the technology advances that have improved our cooking methods. Students will engage in reflection about how people in the past made these particular dishes prior to culinary technological advancements. Students will write a journal reflection describing ways in which technology has helped in the preparation of foods and discuss the benefits of these changes. The teacher should encourage students to identify the connections between science and technology in making these changes possible.

Days 1 & 2

Evaluate

Students' understanding of the methods of heat transfer is assessed through their posters and respective presentations. During the "explain," the teacher should ask questions for further clarification and to check on students' comprehension. At this time, students also have the opportunity to compare and contrast different types of heat transfer as they relate to food preparation.

Culturally Relevant Practices

Academic Success

Whether they present to the whole class or just their neighbor, students should know how to explain the different types of heat transfer and their purposes. When ready to share their posters, the cultural relevance of the poster should be explained along with a verbal description of this dish's specific forms of heat transfer. Being able to successfully teach their classmates demonstrates conceptual understanding beyond recall or comprehension. This is also aligned with the scientific practice of constructing explanations as students need to find out which types of heat transfer are used in the recipes featured and explain it in their own words. Additionally, represent the heat transfer process using a diagram and symbols, which aligns to the practice of "developing and using models." As they present, students utilize these representations to explain the concepts. Students are critically challenged in the completion of this activity. Each recipe has different variations and processes and students are responsible for analyzing and problem-solving to construct a better understanding of the science behind the dish. Once students are more confident in using their critical-thinking and problem-solving skills, they are more likely to continue to challenge themselves within the subject area.

Cultural Competence

This activity asks that students apply what they are learning in class to what they see in their daily lives. Although it may not be pointed out often, conduction, convection, and radiation are everywhere in our kitchens, restaurants, food halls, etc. Many students within this grade level begin cooking or even assisting families in doing so. Many are well aware of how food is heated using an oven, a stovetop, a microwave, and even a grill. This lesson is a great way to get students to draw connections between heat transfers and typical dishes made at home or consumed at restaurants. Not only do students love to share what they have been working on with their classmates, they also enjoy being able to bite into some tasty foods from other cultures present within the classroom. This lesson encourages creativity, collaboration, community, and strong vocabulary, needed by all students to develop academically and culturally. After all, this activity not only feeds student curiosity, but it also fills their bellies.

Mining those Funds of Knowledge!

As students progress in the physical science curriculum, they will have a deeper understanding of how different objects and substances transfer heat between one another. Moreover, heat transfers coincide with the transfer of energy. A particle's kinetic and thermal energy are dependent upon one another, which students would have found through their research while completing this project. For example, students who used a pan and stove in their recipe should understand how a stove gets the pan to heat up by way of increasing the kinetic energy of the pan's particles through conduction.

Students share their funds of knowledge related to food preparation methods. For instance, one dish may have different modes of preparation. However, students may have experienced consuming the dish prepared in different ways and have a preference related to the texture or flavor. They may contribute their expertise in this area when conducting the research and comparing the cooking methods. If students bring dishes to the classroom, they are also incorporating these funds of knowledge and enriching the learning experiences of their classmates.

Questions for Further Consideration

- If students decide to bring dishes to the school, what safety precautions must teachers take into consideration (i.e., food safety, allergies, food intolerance)?
- What are strategies for grouping that teachers should consider to maximize productivity during the collaborative task?

Notes

[1]The link to this resource can be found at http://tinyurl.com/Roman-Oliver-LP.
[2]The link to this resource can be found at http://tinyurl.com/Roman-Oliver-LP.

LESSON PLAN 5.9

Little Star

Perri Lennon

Lesson Title

Little Star

Grade Level/Course

Middle School-Life Science

Suggested Time

Two 60-minute blocks

Learning Objectives

- Students will be able to model how organisms transfer genetic information to determine offspring traits.

Description

This activity introduces students to the endless possibilities of genetics and heredity. Students are tasked with using alleles and Punnett squares to predict the appearance of a baby made by their favorite male and female celebrity.

Next Generation Science Standards

Crosscutting Concepts

- Cause and effect
- Systems and system models

Science and Engineering Practices

- Analyzing and interpreting data
- Developing and using models

Disciplinary Core Ideas

"LS3.B: Variation of Traits—In sexually reproducing organisms, each parent contributes half of the genes acquired (at random) by the offspring. Individuals have two of each chromosome and hence two alleles of each gene, one acquired from each parent. These versions may be identical or may differ from each other." (National Research Council. 2012. *A Framework for K-12 Science Education: Practices, Crosscutting Concepts, and Core Ideas*. Washington, DC: The National Academies Press. https://doi.org/10.17226/13165, p. 160)

5E Lesson

Day 1

Engage

In this activity, students are asked to create a baby using two culturally relevant celebrities of their choice. A week prior to beginning the activity, students are asked to think of three celebrities they believe represent their culture best. The question may be answered by way of group discussion or in writing submitted directly to the teacher. Based on celebrities mentioned in response to the opening query, the teacher will prepare and provide picture cards of all celebrities.

During the first part of the lesson, students are paired based on cultural dissimilarity, to encourage the mutual learning and understanding of one another's culture within the process. Each partner will be responsible for selecting one individual from all celebrities to represent their culture and create a couple—composed of one female and one male. The teacher will keep a celebrity roster and check off the celebrities as the students select them to ensure that there is no repetition of these during the activity.

Explore

Students will create a series of Punnett squares[1] to genetically cross their couple. The picture cards for each celebrity will indicate the specific traits to be crossed. The cards will include the celebrity's alleles for the following genes: nose, eye color, chin, forehead, ears, and dimples. Students will use these to create and utilize their Punnett squares for each of the seven genes. Students should collaborate with their partner to ensure each Punnett square has been accurately completed. Based on their genetic crossing, students should note the probability that each trait be dominant and recessive. It is important that the teacher review student responses for accuracy prior to allowing them to move forward. A series of questions asking the probability of the offspring's specific traits will follow the Punnett square portion. For example, "*What is the probability that the baby will have blue eyes?" "What is the probability that the baby will have a small forehead?"* Using a blank sheet of paper, students should draw their baby based on Punnett square data. The trait with the highest probability should show in the student drawing. If students are to encounter a 50% dominant and a 50% recessive, they may select the trait they would prefer their baby to express. On their paper, they should include the offspring's final genotypes, which should reflect the phenotypes in the illustration. Drawings will not be graded based on aesthetics, but accuracy in that they mirror what the genotypes imply.

Day 2

Explain

During this time, students are allotted a chance to "present" their babies to the class.

Presentations may be brief, but should include the following:

- Explanation from each student as to how the member of the couple they selected represents their culture
- One Punnett square demonstration
- Explanation of the difference between a genotype and a phenotype
- Display and explain how the genotypes reflect in the drawing

Not only does this give students the opportunity to explain the process and demonstrate strategies they use to solve Punnett squares, they are also able to share and explain a piece of their culture. Students listening to the presentations will be encouraged to ask questions about the content or the drawings.

Elaborate

In pairs, students will read the article "Professor Researches Link Between Genetics, Social Media Use."[2] After reading the article, the teacher will ask students to discuss with their classmates their thoughts about the research. After 4 to 5 minutes, students will be asked to voluntarily share some of their ideas with the class. After this discussion, students will be asked to respond to the following prompts in their journals:

- Aside from our physical observable and nonobservable traits, what other traits do you believe may be influenced by our genetic makeup?

- Is there a characteristic about your personality that resembles your mom or your dad? Explain.
- The article (2022) states that "Outside of the genetic factors, the other third of one's social media habits are influenced by social forces: the household environment kids are raised in, what parents teach them about technology and interpersonal communication, peer and teacher influence, and so on" (para. 5). Which of these factors do you believe is more influential in the way you interact with social media? Why do you think this is the case?

Days 1 & 2

Evaluate

Students are evaluated at different stages during the lesson. Their understanding about how to use Punnett squares and their ability to successfully cross two individuals is evaluated during the "explore" and "explain." Completion of the Punnett squares, in addition to determining the probability of each genotype and phenotype, is aligned with the NGSS standards. As students explain how the drawing of their "babies" represents the features observed in the Punnett squares, the teacher assesses how well students can connect the concept of genotype and phenotype.

Culturally Relevant Practices

Academic Success

The first piece of the activity requires that students know and understand the difference between a phenotype—physical appearance—and a genotype—genetic makeup—which they must compare and contrast based on the information provided on the picture cards. Students must discuss and agree upon at least three similarities and differences between their celebrities physically. It is not guaranteed that students will be able to find similarities or differences between their couple's genotypes; they must still examine and investigate accordingly. Students are also tasked with utilizing a model, the Punnett square, to demonstrate the genetic crosses and their outcome. Students analyze and interpret the data in their Punnett squares to answer the questions related to genotypic and phenotypic frequency. Finally, during the "elaborate," students are asked to share their views related to an article on the link between genetics and the use of social media. This portion of the lesson promotes critical thinking and reflection through discussion and their journal writing.

Cultural Competence

Many students often engage in conversations during class about their favorite actors, singers, or sports figures. They follow them on social media, watch them on TV or their favorite streaming platform, and sometimes even try to dress or talk like them. This lesson gives them an opportunity to consider how genetic traits are observed in these celebrities that they admire. The lesson also intentionally groups students with different ethnicities or backgrounds to encourage collaboration across cultures. In doing this, students have an opportunity to discuss physical traits that are representative of them.

Mining those Funds of Knowledge!

Students' funds of knowledge related to popular celebrities are incorporated in this lesson. As mentioned above, students use their knowledge to engage in discussions and incorporate scientific practices in a way that adds relevance. When students calculate the genotype and phenotype frequencies, they make decisions about the traits that will be represented in their drawings. The drawing activity gives students an opportunity to utilize their art skills to sketch the babies as well.

Questions for Further Consideration

- What are potential biases that teachers must be aware of in preparing the materials for this lesson?
- What alternatives to whole-class presentations should the teacher consider?

Notes

[1] The link to this resource can be found at http://tinyurl.com/Roman-Oliver-LP.
[2] The link to this resource can be found at http://tinyurl.com/Roman-Oliver-LP.

References

Ladson-Billings, G. (1995). But that's just good teaching! The case for culturally relevant pedagogy. *Theory Into Practice*, *34*(3), 159–165.

National Research Council. (2012). *A framework for K-12 science education: Practices, crosscutting concepts, and core ideas*. The National Academies Press. https://doi.org/10.17226/13165

NGSS Lead States. (2013). *Next Generation Science Standards: For states, by states*. The National Academies Press.

Professor researches link between genetics, social media use. (2022). Retrieved from https://www.kent.edu/mdj/news/professor-researches-link-between-genetics-social-media-use#:~:text=Specifically%2C%20he%20found%20that%20about,he%20or%20she%20is%20born

SIX

Lessons by the Author

THE NEXT SECTION FEATURES LESSON plans that I used as a high school teacher to connect students' culture with the science content. I have revised these to adapt them to the structure of the chapters. The lessons follow the same structure as in Chapter 5. Two biology and two physical sciences lesson plans are featured. In the same way as with the previous lessons, these can be easily modified for middle school students.

At the end of the book, there is a short autobiography that features all contributors. The purpose of this was for each teacher to share more about their background and teaching context. While the autobiography section includes my information, I wanted to provide some additional context for my teaching experience and share a little about the students I taught during my 12 years at the high school. As I mentioned at the start of the book, I taught English Language Learners for most of those 12 years. While my practices were not precisely culturally relevant at the start, I was later exposed to the framework and became passionate about incorporating students' culture in the classroom towards the last few years of my teaching career. The students I taught came from different parts of the world (i.e., Mexico, Bangladesh, Brazil, Iran, Guatemala, and other countries). Many of them recently moved to the United States; therefore, their English skills were limited. Due to this, students were enrolled in the English to Speakers of Other Languages (ESOL) program at the district. However, after several years, and based on their English performance, sometimes students exited the program. Because of this, I had a wide array of English skills represented in the classroom, in addition to the cultural differences. This allowed me to incorporate varied grouping strategies for different purposes. While students came from different parts of the world, most of them were from Spanish-speaking countries. As a native Spanish speaker myself, I was able to communicate with most of my students in their language if needed. However, I understood that students needed to develop their English skills, so even when I had a group of students who all spoke Spanish, I would still use English to teach the whole class and create the materials and activities. In a way, I believe that speaking their language gave me an advantage in terms of building trust and developing positive relationships with my students.

LESSON PLAN 6.1

Renewable Sources of Energy Around the World

Lesson Title

Renewable Sources of Energy Around the World

Grade Level/Course

High School-Environmental Science

Suggested Time

Two 90-minute blocks

Learning Objective

- Students will be able to explain the advantages and disadvantages of the different types of renewable sources of energy.

Description

This lesson is an introduction to renewable sources of energy. There are different types of energy sources that are considered renewable, such as solar, wind, geothermal, and hydroelectric. Students will be exposed to the different types and given the opportunity to research how different countries utilize these renewable sources.

Next Generation Science Standards

Crosscutting Concepts

- Energy and matter
- Cause and effect

Science and Engineering Practices

- Constructing explanations and designing solutions
- Obtaining, evaluating, and communicating information

Disciplinary Core Ideas

"ESS3.A: Natural Resources—Energy and fuels that humans use are derived from natural sources, and their use affects the environment in multiple ways. Some resources are renewable over time, and others are not." (National Research Council. 2012. *A Framework for K-12 Science Education: Practices, Crosscutting Concepts, and Core Ideas.* Washington, DC: The National Academies Press. https://doi.org/10.17226/13165, p. 192)

5E Lesson

Day 1

Engage

The teacher will share the following: Growing up in Puerto Rico, we did not own a dryer. This is still the case for many households there. Why do you think this is? Students will be asked to think about this and then discuss with their elbow partner. The teacher will then ask some students to voluntarily share their thoughts. The teacher will then ask students to think about one activity that was different in terms of how they used energy back in their countries. Students will write this down and compare it with how that activity or activities are different in the United States. The teacher will ask students to share voluntarily as well. The teacher will then explain that today's lesson will focus on exploring renewable sources of energy. The teacher will ask students what they think "renewable" means. After students share, the teacher will write a formal definition on the board using their ideas, adding or revising as needed. The teacher may break down the word into its different parts to facilitate interpretation (i.e., "re"-"new"-"able"). Translating dictionaries (i.e., Spanish, Farsi, Portuguese, etc.) will be available for students that need a direct translation as well.

Explore

The class will be divided into six groups. Each group will be tasked with exploring how one specific country utilizes a different type of renewable energy source (from the list below).

- Solar
- Wind
- Hydroelectric

- Tidal
- Geothermal
- Biomass

Students will be asked to research the following:

- How does this type of renewable source of energy work? (How is energy obtained from the source?)
- What are the advantages and disadvantages of using this type of energy?
- How does (country assigned) capture and utilize this source of energy?

The teacher will provide a list of websites[1] to direct students. Students will also be directed to different websites that demonstrate, using interactive ways, how energy is produced using this renewable source.

During the remainder of the class, students will work in groups to research these questions and create a product (e.g., poster, article, presentation, video) to share this information with the class the next day.

Note: The teacher may use different grouping strategies. Students may be grouped based on interest (by allowing them to choose the type of energy they would like to research) or the teacher may create heterogeneous groups in terms of background/ethnicity.

Day 2

Explain

Groups will present their respective renewable sources of energy and discuss how each country is optimizing these. As each group presents, the other students will take notes on the advantages and disadvantages of each type of renewable source of energy.

Elaborate

Students will select one renewable source of energy that would be optimal for use in their countries of origin. They will complete a Claims-Evidence-Reasoning (CER) template[2] identifying this type of energy and providing evidence, based on their experience and background knowledge (students may opt to conduct further research or consult with their parents/relatives as well). Within the reasoning section, students will strengthen their claim by discussing how the evidence supports their choice. The CER is mainly a writing task but can be used as the precursor for discursive or argumentative activities (i.e., debates, Socratic seminars). This will be turned in as homework the next day.

Days 1 & 2

Evaluate

Evaluation occurs at different stages of the 5E cycle. For example, pre-assessment occurs during the "engage" as students share their responses with each other and the class. During the "explore," students are asked questions to assess their understanding when conducting the research. Teachers may use a rubric during the "explain" section to ensure that students have answered the assigned questions correctly. During this stage as well, students' collaboration and creative skills can also be evaluated (if this is part of the criteria that teachers choose for the assignment). Finally, teachers should also ask questions during this stage to check on comprehension. Writing and argumentation skills are evaluated during the "elaborate" stage.

Culturally Relevant Practices

Academic Success

This lesson engages students in research and analysis of information. This may include data analysis to determine how advantageous a source of energy is when compared to another. Students are expected to "obtain, evaluate, and communicate" this information, so that other students can learn about the different types of renewable energy sources. Evaluating findings from research requires students to assess the reliability of the source. Strategies to do this should be taught explicitly before students engage in research, especially when using online sources. During the "elaborate" stage, students are constructing explanations about their chosen energy source using the CER framework. All these activities represent the NGSS Scientific Practices #6-"Constructing explanations" and #8-"Obtaining, evaluating, and communicating information."

Cultural Competence

Collaborative learning gives students an opportunity to share and be exposed to different ideas and points of view. Allowing students to present their findings during the "explain" using different formats gives them an opportunity to utilize and showcase their unique skills and abilities. Students are tasked with identifying characteristics of their everyday lives before migrating to the United States during the "engage." Additionally, students bring back this cultural knowledge when completing the CER, as it is necessary to evaluate the effectiveness of the energy source in their countries of origin. They utilize other resources (e.g., websites, parents) to elaborate in these areas as well. Identifying what the ideal energy source would be for their native countries requires them to recall their experiences. Students are encouraged to discuss these ideas with their parents as well, which may enrich their narratives and rationale. All these skills are necessary as they explore the value of using specific renewable sources of energy.

Critical Consciousness

During the CER activity, students engage in reflection about the advantages and disadvantages of the selected source of energy. This critical examination allows them to go beyond the comprehension and analysis of the different types. They are asked to discuss the value of using renewable sources of energy. Teachers should ask probing questions to facilitate a discussion of how these sources of energy may be the solution to current environmental issues. Students evaluate how these energy sources are utilized in other countries and engage in critique or examination of current practices in the United States. The teacher should ask: "Why are these sources of energy only utilized in some areas?" "Why are only some people benefitting from these?" These questions help develop critical consciousness in students.

Mining those Funds of Knowledge!

There are several opportunities to draw students' funds of knowledge within this lesson. During the "engage," students are asked to consider a scenario and respond to it. This requires them to draw on previous experiences and ideas related to the topic. When asked to identify the example from their countries, students can contribute their unique background knowledge to the discussion. When students engage in the CER, they draw from their life experiences in their countries of origin and from their knowledge of everyday activities to support their claims.

Questions for Further Consideration

- What information about students' background should teachers consider when planning the lesson to maximize the incorporation of funds of knowledge?
- What misconceptions may students bring into the lesson that need to be addressed before the "exploration"?
- How could teachers ensure that students have the necessary resources to conduct the research required?

Notes

[1]The link to this resource can be found at http://tinyurl.com/Roman-Oliver-LP.
[2]The link to this resource can be found at http://tinyurl.com/Roman-Oliver-LP.

References

Ladson-Billings, G. (1995). But that's just good teaching! The case for culturally relevant pedagogy. Theory Into Practice, 34(3), 159–165.

National Research Council. (2012). *A framework for K-12 science education: Practices, crosscutting concepts, and core ideas.* The National Academies Press. https://doi.org/10.17226/13165

NGSS Lead States. (2013). Next Generation Science Standards: For states, by states. The National Academies Press.

LESSON PLAN 6.2

Sport Injuries

Lesson Title
Sport Injuries

Grade Level/Course
High School-Biology

Suggested Time
Two 90-minute blocks

Learning Objectives

- Students will be able to describe how the muscular and nervous systems interact to produce motion and respond to injuries.

Description
This lesson is an introduction to the muscular and nervous systems and how they depend on each other. Students will be exposed to the nature of some sports injuries. They will also explore the functions of these two systems and how they interact and rely on each other to produce motion.

Next Generation Science Standards

Crosscutting Concepts

- Stability and change
- Structure and function
- Systems and system models

Science and Engineering Practices

- Constructing explanations and designing solutions
- Obtaining, evaluating, and communicating information
- Developing and using models

Disciplinary Core Ideas
"LS1.A: Structure and Function—Systems of specialized cells within organisms help them perform the essential functions of life." (National Research

Council. 2012. *A Framework for K-12 Science Education: Practices, Crosscutting Concepts, and Core Ideas*. Washington, DC: The National Academies Press. https://doi.org/10.17226/13165, p. 145)

5E Lesson

Day 1

Engage

Students will be asked about which sports or physical activities they like to practice. They are then asked to recall if they have ever experienced an injury related to sports or a physical activity. Perhaps they have not personally, but know of someone that has. Students are asked to share in their groups (4–5 each) first. After a few minutes, the teacher facilitates a discussion asking students to share what caused the injury and how they recovered. The teacher may choose to play a video about sport injuries.

Explore

The teacher will share the following resource[1] with students. Students will work in groups to investigate one common sports injury described in the resource. Students may choose to use other resources as well. They will be tasked with identifying the causes, describing the symptoms and recovery options. They will be asked to connect their experience with any of these injuries (or related ones), to the information presented in the different resources. Students will create a short visual presentation to share with the class at the end.

Day 2

Explain

The teacher will overview the role and functions of the muscular system, as well as the nervous system, paying attention to how these are connected when playing sports. Students will be provided with a handout displaying diagrams of both systems. They will identify and label the main areas/regions in the nervous system, as well as the main muscles. The teacher will ask each group to locate the areas impacted by the injury that they researched yesterday.

Elaborate

Students will be given additional time after the lecture to finalize their presentations and add any information that is relevant based on what the teacher covered. The students will share their presentations to the class highlighting their own experiences as it relates to the injuries. After the presentations, students will create a concept map illustrating how movement is regulated by interactions between the nervous and muscular system.

After this, the teacher will present some statistics on brain injuries from different sports.[2] The teacher will pose the following question: "Do you think that there should be more regulations in sports, both in school and in colleges, to prevent brain injuries?" The students will have a few minutes to discuss this with their research partners. After about 5 minutes, students will answer this question in their journals. They will justify their response using the content from the lesson and their views on how organizations should approach this issue.

Days 1 & 2

Evaluate

Evaluation occurs at different stages of the 5E cycle. For example, pre-assessment occurs during the "engage" when students' understanding of injuries is shared through the class discussion. During the "explore," students are connecting the research with their own experiences. During the "elaborate," students' concept maps may be evaluated to assess if they understand the connection between the two systems and how they work. Finally, the writing piece allows teachers an opportunity to identify any misconceptions related to the learning experience and evaluate students' use of academic language in their writing.

Culturally Relevant Practices

Academic Success

During the "elaborate," students create a concept map that serves as a model to illustrate the dependance of both systems. Students demonstrate their comprehension of the concepts through the use of the graphic organizer. Additionally, through the use of the diagram of the different body systems, students demonstrate the interaction between these to produce movement.

This connects with the NGSS standard. Students also practice research skills and interpret data in order to create their presentations.

Cultural Competence

Sports is an important part of students' culture. Many of them are involved in different types of sports, whether outside of school or as part of a team. Even for students that are not involved in playing a sport, they typically engage in conversations about past games during class or wear fan apparel to school. Watching games as a family is an important tradition in many U.S. homes as well. Sports events have the power to bring a community together and have an impact on different aspects of everyday life. Through this activity, students have an opportunity to connect this part of their lives to the science content.

Critical Consciousness

During the "elaborate," students are invited to share their views about the responsibilities that organizations should have in preventing sport injuries. The statistics shown by the teacher may initially shock students. The teacher may also use additional resources[3] and/or videos that feature real cases to help students develop their arguments related to this issue. These activities engage students in critical thinking and in analyzing how different factors may impact how injuries are prevented and addressed.

Mining those Funds of Knowledge!

Students' funds of knowledge are drawn mainly during the "engage" and "elaborate" stages. As students share about their participation in sports and past injuries, they use their background knowledge and experiences to enrich the class discussion. They also share about the specific injury symptoms and how to care for these from a personal point of view during the "elaborate." Some of the information presented in the resource may be expounded on by these previous experiences, which allows students to utilize their expertise when teaching others about it. This increases students' sense of agency of the material as well.

Questions for Further Consideration

- What are some physical activities that teachers should consider when planning the lesson to maximize students' use of background knowledge?
- What additional resources may teachers locate beforehand to guide students during the research portion?
- How could teachers ensure that students collaborate effectively during the "explore"?

Notes

[1]The link to this resource can be found at http://tinyurl.com/Roman-Oliver-LP.
[2]The link to this resource can be found at http://tinyurl.com/Roman-Oliver-LP.
[3]The link to this resource can be found at http://tinyurl.com/Roman-Oliver-LP.

References

Ladson-Billings, G. (1995). But that's just good teaching! The case for culturally relevant pedagogy. *Theory Into Practice*, *34*(3), 159–165.

National Research Council. (2012). *A framework for K-12 science education: Practices, crosscutting concepts, and core ideas*. The National Academies Press. https://doi.org/10.17226/13165

NGSS Lead States. (2013). *Next Generation Science Standards: For states, by states*. The National Academies Press.

LESSON PLAN 6.3

Exploring Friction

Lesson Title
Exploring Friction

Grade Level/Course
High School-Physical Sciences

Suggested Time
Two 90-minute blocks

Lesson Objectives

- Students will be able to identify factors that contribute to an increase or decrease in the different types of friction.

Description
This lesson is an introduction to the different types of friction (i.e., static, sliding, and rolling). Students will engage in hands-on exploration to understand how friction impacts motion. Additionally, students will connect these ideas with how different shoes are used for specific sports and activities.

Next Generation Science Standards

Crosscutting Concepts

- Cause and effect
- Scale, proportion, and quantity

Science and Engineering Practices

- Analyzing and interpreting data

Disciplinary Core Ideas
"PS1.A: Structure and Properties of Matter—The structure and interactions of matter at the bulk scale are determined by electrical forces within and between atoms." (National Research Council. 2012. *A Framework for K-12 Science Education: Practices, Crosscutting Concepts, and Core Ideas*. Washington, DC: The National Academies Press. https://doi.org/10.17226/13165, p. 109)

5E Lesson

Day 1

Engage

The teacher will engage students in a Think-Pair-Share activity. First, students will be instructed to open a bottle using their hands. Then, they will be instructed to either put lotion or oil on their hands. Then they will be asked to try to open the bottle again. Students will individually think about what they observed/experienced for one minute. They may write down any thoughts they have about their observations. Then, they will turn to a partner and share their ideas about the observations they made. Finally, the teacher will call out some pairs to share their thoughts.

Explore

Guided Inquiry-Students will be provided with different types of surfaces, wooden blocks with hooks, and spring scales. Students will be asked the following question: "How does the type of surface affect the movement of an object?" They will work in groups of four to design an experiment to answer this question. They should use the materials provided as well as any other materials available in the classroom, as needed. They may use blocks of different sizes and shapes, as well as different surfaces to measure the force required to move these using the spring scales. Students will create a document with the procedure, observations, and data section completed, as well as a formulated response to the main question.

Day 2

Explain

The teacher overviews the three types of friction: static, sliding, and rolling. As these concepts are introduced, connections are made with the stations activity. Additionally, questions should be asked to ensure that students can identify the different types of friction using the examples from the stations as well as everyday examples in general. The students will complete a tree map (thinking map[1]) by identifying each type of friction, describing it, and providing an example or picture.

Elaborate

Students will be asked to consider the applications of this knowledge in different areas. The teacher should ask students where they see friction acting on objects every day. How is it helpful? How is it not? The teacher will continue to provide examples, but guide students into thinking about sports. The teacher may ask how we see friction in sports. The teacher may need to prompt students into considering how the shoes are used in different types of sports and other physical activities (i.e., hiking, rollerblading, bowling) and how they work with the surfaces they encounter. The teacher will ask students to choose a sport or physical activity based on a list provided. Based on the students' selections, they will be placed in groups to investigate how the type of shoe used is appropriate for the type of surface where the activity takes place. Students may conduct research online[2] to look at the characteristics of the shoes as well as the surface. They will make observations and complete a CER template.[3] Their claim will be one of the following: The type of shoe used in (type of activity), (increases/decreases) friction. They will provide evidence for their claim using their observations and any other relevant experiences (including practicing the activity). Finally, in their reasoning, the students will explain how their claim is supported by the science concepts that they have explored.

Days 1 & 2

Evaluate

Evaluation of students' learning takes place at different times throughout the lesson. For example, students' previous ideas about the concept of friction are assessed during the "engage" without formally introducing the term. The teacher may notice if the students are using related key terms such as "force," "effort," "increase," or "decrease." Students' understanding of the concept is further assessed through the laboratory question. Additionally, their ability to write a hypothesis and procedure for the lab is evaluated at this point. Finally, through the CER, students' analysis skills are assessed as they are required to explain what happens to the friction when utilizing certain types of footwear for each sport.

Culturally Relevant Practices

Academic Success

This lesson engages students in guided inquiry. This is one of the highest levels of inquiry, characterized by teachers posing a question and tasking students with designing an experiment to answer it. Students engage in several science and engineering practices during the laboratory activity, including "planning and carrying out investigations" as well as "analyzing and interpreting data." During the "explain," students organize information from the teacher's lecture using a thinking map. This allows for them to have a visual representation of the types of friction through the examples. During the "elaborate" stage, students construct explanations about how friction is increased or decreased in certain sports or activities through the use of different types of shoes. The CER framework engages students in argumentation and practice of scientific writing.

Cultural Competence

In this lesson, students are again engaged in collaborative learning which allows them opportunities to discuss their ideas and observations. They engage in collaboration during all stages of the 5E model, except the "explain." Students are also responsible for designing a lab activity to answer a teacher-posed question. As they discuss their ideas with their group, students can utilize their previous experience in related areas, including any activities that involve friction. Some students have worked in their family's construction business and understand some of the principles related to surfaces and friction. Through the CER, students may utilize their knowledge of sports, physical activities, and gear. Many of the students in class play soccer or football and understand that the right shoes can make a significant difference in performance.

Mining those Funds of Knowledge!

Students contribute their funds of knowledge to the lesson mainly during the "explore" and "elaborate" sections. As students design their laboratories they are using their previous knowledge of science, as well as their ideas on how to investigate each type of friction. They may draw on their past experiences working with any of the materials available in other areas as well. Many students work in construction, for example, and may have knowledge of certain surfaces that increase friction. Many students also practice soccer or football and either wear or are familiar with the footwear used in these sports. They may contribute to the "reasoning" section of the CER based on their own experiences practicing the sport or activity.

Questions for Further Consideration

- What are some safety considerations that teachers should plan for during the "engage"?
- How could the level of inquiry during the "explore" be increased even further?
- What are some other grouping strategies that may be used during the "elaborate" (besides selection of sport)?

Notes

[1] The link to this resource can be found at http://tinyurl.com/Roman-Oliver-LP.
[2] The link to this resource can be found at http://tinyurl.com/Roman-Oliver-LP.
[3] The link to this resource can be found at http://tinyurl.com/Roman-Oliver-LP.

References

Ladson-Billings, G. (1995). But that's just good teaching! The case for culturally relevant pedagogy. *Theory Into Practice, 34*(3), 159–165.

National Research Council. (2012). *A framework for K-12 science education: Practices, crosscutting concepts, and core ideas*. The National Academies Press. https://doi.org/10.17226/13165

NGSS Lead States. (2013). *Next Generation Science Standards: For states, by states*. The National Academies Press.

LESSON PLAN 6.4

Genetically Modified Foods

Lesson Title
Genetically Modified Foods

Grade Level/Course
High School-Biology

Suggested Time
Two 90-minute blocks

Lesson Objective

- Students will be able to evaluate the advantages and disadvantages of the use of genetic engineering in foods.

Description
This lesson explores the use of genetic engineering in crops in the last few decades. The students have an opportunity to discuss the advantages and disadvantages of genetically modified foods, or GMOs, through a Socratic seminar. The students also engage in critical thinking and the practice of argumentation skills through a debate.

Next Generation Science Standards

Crosscutting Concepts

- Cause and effect

Science and Engineering Practices

- Obtaining, evaluating, and communicating information
- Engaging in argument from evidence

Disciplinary Core Ideas
"LS4.B: Natural Selection—In *artificial* selection, humans have the capacity to influence certain characteristics of organisms by selective breeding. One can choose desired parental traits determined by genes, which are then passed onto offspring." (National Research Council. 2012. *A Framework for K-12 Science*

Education: Practices, Crosscutting Concepts, and Core Ideas. Washington, DC: The National Academies Press. https://doi.org/10.17226/13165, p. 164)

5E Lesson

Day 1

Engage

The teacher will ask students to think about their favorite fruit. After about a minute, the teacher will ask students to share with their elbow partner their response and explain why this is their favorite fruit. The teacher will show students pictures of organic versus genetically modified fruits (GMOs). The teacher will ask students to guess which one is organic versus GMO. Ask students, "Aside from the way they look, how else can you tell the difference between these?"

Explore

The teacher will divide the class in pairs. Students will work together to research the history of GMOs, as well as the pros and cons. Students will use different resources[1] provided by the teacher as well as valid and reliable sources of their choice.

Day 2

Explain

Students will participate in a Socratic seminar to share their ideas about GMOs after conducting the research. During the seminar, students should take notes of important ideas on both sides. The teacher will facilitate the seminar by asking the following questions throughout:

- *Do you believe using genetic engineering in foods is necessary? Why or why not?*
- *Which of the advantages of GMOs is more convincing of the need for these?*
- *Which of the disadvantages of GMOs is most concerning to you as a consumer?*
- *Do you or your family prefer to purchase/consume organic or GMO products? Explain.*

- *How does the quality of the dishes that your family prepares change because of genetic engineering?*
- *If cost was not an issue, would you only consume organic products? Why or why not?*

Elaborate

Now that students have had an opportunity to discuss the advantages and disadvantages of GMOs, the teacher will have students choose a side of the argument. Students will write arguments in favor of or against GMOs in preparation for a debate. Additionally, students will list several possible counterarguments. They will write statements to refute these in preparation for the debate. After this, the teacher will select five participants from each group to present their arguments and facilitate the debate. After the debate, the rest of the class will select the group that has presented and supported their arguments more successfully.

Days 1 & 2

Evaluate

Evaluation occurs at different stages of the 5E cycle. During the "explore," students are engaging in research/investigation of the topic. The teacher may have a rubric or checklist to evaluate students' skills related to selecting trustworthy resources and summarizing important ideas. During the "explain," the teacher evaluates students' understanding of genetic engineering as well as its applications through the use of the listed open-ended questions. Finally, the debate gives teachers an opportunity to evaluate students' argumentation skills.

Culturally Relevant Practices

Academic Success

Students are engaged in research and investigating genetic engineering and its applications. They utilize this information to choose to be in favor of or against these practices. These activities allow students to practice writing, communicating, and arguing using scientific academic language.

Cultural Competence

During the Socratic seminar, students are able to share the value of certain food products in their own cultures. Authentic cuisine from different parts of the world utilizes mainly organic ingredients. Farming techniques have changed significantly throughout the last few years. However, every country does not necessarily use the same technology that is used in the United States. When students bring in their cultural knowledge about what makes their food special, both in terms of the ingredients used and their preparation, teachers are opening the space for them to utilize their funds of knowledge.

Critical Consciousness

When students are asked "If cost wasn't an issue, would you only consume organic products? Why or why not?", there is an opportunity to analyze the use of GMOs using a critical lens. It is well known that organic products are significantly more expensive than GMOs. We could argue that, if there are more disadvantages than advantages to using genetic engineering in foods, those that cannot afford organic products are affected. Students are encouraged to dive into this issue and consider possible ways to make organic products more affordable.

Mining those Funds of Knowledge!

There are a few opportunities to draw on students' funds of knowledge within this lesson. During the "explain," students have a chance to share about the value of food and the ingredients used to prepare these, based on their own cultural background and family traditions. This is an opportunity for them to showcase what they know and even share any skills related to cooking or preparing food. During the "elaborate," students can utilize their argumentation skills. There are not many opportunities to engage in argumentation in science. Therefore, students may draw on skills developed in other classes such as English language arts or social studies.

Questions for Further Consideration

- What are some things that teachers should consider when planning the lesson to maximize students' use of background knowledge?

- What misconceptions about genetic engineering may students bring into the lesson that need to be addressed before the "exploration"?
- Which grouping strategies are more effective for the "explore"?

Notes

[1]The link to this resource can be found at http://tinyurl.com/Roman-Oliver-LP.

References

Ladson-Billings, G. (1995). But that's just good teaching! The case for culturally relevant pedagogy. *Theory Into Practice*, *34*(3), 159–165.

National Research Council. (2012). *A framework for K-12 science education: Practices, crosscutting concepts, and core ideas*. The National Academies Press. https://doi.org/10.17226/13165

NGSS Lead States. (2013). *Next Generation Science Standards: For states, by states*. The National Academies Press.

PART III

NEXT STEPS—BECOMING A CULTURALLY RELEVANT SCIENCE TEACHER

SEVEN

Ten Best Practices for Incorporating Culturally Relevant Pedagogy in the Science Classroom

I WANTED TO INCLUDE A SECTION that outlined some best practices that I have learned throughout my almost 20 years as an educator, when it comes to being a culturally relevant teacher. Some of these may be found in education literature in this area, of course. However, I thought it would help to add my own experiences and insights on each.

Get to know your students

One of the most common expressions I hear from my students about the difficulty to implement CRP is that "it is impossible to know everything about the cultures of all students." Somehow, they have concluded that, in order to be a culturally relevant teacher, you need to understand all the cultures represented in your classroom. While this could not be farther from the truth, teachers are quick to give up on the idea of cultural relevance, given how overwhelmingly diverse their classrooms are these days. The premise of CRP is that teachers will create learning experiences that promote academic success, develop cultural competence, and foster critical consciousness. There is no requirement to conduct in-depth research about each of the cultures in order to design lessons that are culturally relevant to the students. There is, however, a need for teachers to be curious and make an effort to get to know their students. This is not a superficial "getting to know," as in finding out where they are from or what their favorite type of food is. This goes beyond the surface and into what students' goals are and what they care about. While some books suggest different ways of doing this, there are a few strategies that I believe are very powerful, not only to get to know students, but to demonstrate care. This, as Hammond's book, *Culturally Responsive Teaching and the Brain* suggests, can make the difference between creating a culturally responsive learning environment or not (2014).

The following are strategies that many of my former and current students have also implemented with success.

- Student surveys: You may be able to find different examples of student interest surveys online. However, my recommendation is that you create one to find out what you would like to know about your students. You may gather ideas from an online resource, but I suggest you revise the questions to tailor them to your needs. One typical question we could include is "What are your hobbies or interests?" This question can reveal a lot about the type of learner that you are working with. I also recommend that some of these questions are related to the content you teach, or even better, to the units you will be covering during the school semester or year. For instance, one question I liked to ask my students was to describe their feelings about science. I wanted them to be open and honest about past experiences with science classes or their overall demeanor towards the subject. While questions like these can be structured to be answered as a multiple choice or through a Likert scale, we should also include open-ended questions for students to share the whys of their responses. Ideally, these surveys are administered during the first week of school, so that teachers have an opportunity to use the data when planning their lessons and activities throughout the year.
- Demonstrating interest in students' lives outside the classroom: Many of my students, who are teacher candidates, are intentional about finding out what matters to their students outside of the classroom. You may find out through the interest survey that one of your students is on the soccer team at school. You may then decide that you want to engage in some conversation with this student about soccer. However, what seems to have even more power in demonstrating that you care as a teacher is to attend some of these games. Furthermore, teachers that go out of their way to meet parents during these events share how much of a difference this makes. It promotes collaboration and support, strengthening the relationship between parents and the school learning environment.
- Provide ample opportunities for classroom discourse: During my 12 years of K-12 teaching, I loved being able to hear students talk about their experiences or share their ideas about a topic in science. One

practice I implemented often was Socratic seminars. While I share more about this strategy later in this section, these structured discourse opportunities allowed students to freely communicate their views about a topic and learn from each other. While a survey may give us information about a student that is responsible for cooking for her siblings at home or another that works in construction during the weekends, the seminar allowed me to take a deeper look into what this meant for each of them. I was able to discover what they cared about, what frustrated them, what their passions were, and what they dreamed to accomplish. Furthermore, this gave me an opportunity to show care and compassion, as well as challenge them to envision how things could be different. This is an important part of becoming critically conscious.

Become a learner

When I was a science teacher, I would often tell my students that I learned more from them than what they could ever learn from me. This seemed to puzzle them, but I made an effort to explicitly point out each time they taught me something new. Along with this, the message that we do not know everything was one they needed to hear.

The evolution of the science classroom, from a mostly teacher-centered to a student-centered environment, exemplifies this type of thinking. A classroom in which most of the teaching is still done through lectures or whole-group discussions has not embraced the idea that students' background knowledge and skills are as valuable as (if not more than) the content that teachers are planning to present. Teachers that have discovered this idea design lessons that not only draw on students' knowledge, but capitalize on these to enrich the learning experience of all involved. In order to do this, the teacher needs to be able to see themself as a learner in the process.

An important part of adopting the role of a learner in the classroom is to acknowledge students' funds of knowledge. We explored this idea throughout the book and looked into some examples of ways to do this within each lesson. Beyond inviting students to share their knowledge and expertise in the science classroom, the teacher should also recognize the dynamic nature of science content. Science is constantly changing. While many of its theories and laws have been tested and taught for centuries, new research and technology is continually adding to this body of knowledge. Additionally, what it means to "do science" has changed significantly from a few decades ago. Students' knowledge about some of the topics we teach may be different than what we learned during our education courses, but it may be more accurate if they have been recently exposed to new research and findings in the area.

When teachers adopt the role of learners, they seek to grow. We are familiar with the phrase "teachers never stop learning." This is not just in reference to ever-changing content, but to learning about new strategies that enhance students' classroom experiences. While many teachers seek graduate degrees or professional development opportunities to accomplish this, there are some that are reflective practitioners and continuously seek to improve their craft. Whether it is through attending science education conferences, becoming an avid reader of research in this area, or partnering with other teachers, growing as an educator is imperative. Not only will this help you develop skills to meet the needs of all your students, but it will demonstrate to them the value of being a lifelong learner. We are not just teachers; we are role models.

Develop agency

Ladson-Billings' framework emphasizes the importance of developing student agency, both in and out of the classroom. This is exemplified in the actions of one of the teachers that was part of her study.

> Lewis, a White woman [sic], recognized that the African American boys possessed social power. Rather than allow that power to influence their peers in negative ways, Lewis challenged the boys to demonstrate academic power by drawing on issues and ideas they found meaningful. As the boys began to take on academic leadership, other students saw this as a positive trait and developed similar behaviors. Instead of entering into antagonistic relationships with the boys, Lewis found ways to value their skills and abilities and channel them in academically important ways. (1995, p. 160)

Agency can be exhibited in other areas of the classroom, in addition to positioning students as leaders. Students should be given opportunities to have a say or choose from an array of ways to demonstrate their learning, for example. This is also a characteristic of culturally responsive teaching (Gay, 2018).

As we discussed earlier, students may also be given opportunities to provide feedback about the strategies that are more effective in helping them learn. This can be done at different stages of the learning process. When teachers use these data to improve their teaching, students see the value of using their agency to effect change in the classroom.

Shift the power dynamic

One of the main areas of concern for new teachers is classroom management. While many books have been written about it and entire courses are devoted to equipping teachers with effective strategies, teachers still experience many challenges within this area. In their first year, some adopt the roles of authoritarians, while others are too permissive. Neither of these extremes seems to do the trick when it comes to establishing and maintaining a positive learning environment. This is not to say that there is one method that always works. However, there is some foundational work that needs to happen in order to set the tone for success when it comes to classroom management.

Zaretta Hammond, in *Culturally Responsive Teaching and the Brain*, talks about how focusing on building relationships should be the teacher's priority. Additionally, as we previously discussed, giving students agency in different parts of the learning process can have a positive effect in their ability to regulate their behavior (2014). While the teacher should still be the authority figure in the classroom, students can be invited to be a part of the decision making at different times. This is what we refer to as shifting the power dynamics.

One of my favorite strategies to use as a teacher was Socratic seminars. There was something unique about sitting in a circle together and being able to see each other when sharing our ideas. The teachers sit at the same level as the students, which positions them as a participant, and learner, in the conversation. The teacher has some prepared questions and facilitates the discussion with these, but invites students to also ask questions of each other, build on their classmates' answers, and pose new ideas. Imagine if all classes were held this way. Teachers acting as facilitators, rather than experts in their field, eager to learn about what their students think about an issue or topic. Students exercise agency through the exchange of ideas and through co-facilitating by asking follow-up questions.

Barton worked with students from low SES whose parents had to work in the evenings. Due to this, these middle and high school students had to act as caretakers for younger siblings, having to take the lead in many household tasks. Barton discussed how difficult it was for students to shift from being leaders at home, to passive consumers of knowledge in the classroom (2003). As we discussed in the previous section, finding ways to help students develop these leadership skills while at school may be necessary. In a way, these skills represent students' funds of knowledge as they are part of their upbringing and social contexts.

Foster collaboration

Cooperative and collaborative learning have been buzzwords in education for many decades now. However, teachers' ideas about what effective collaboration in the classroom looks like differ significantly. Most seasoned educators understand that this goes beyond having students work "in groups." We need to be intentional about the goals for choosing to do this. In other words, we need to identify learning objectives that go beyond the cognitive development we aim to foster by addressing gains expected through the collaborative process. These objectives and goals should be clear for us, but also be made explicit for students before engaging in collaboration. When covering this topic in my teacher education courses, I typically ask students to share their best practices in this area. Below is a collection of what has worked for them, with some rationale based on their collective experience and my insights.

- Establish and overview expectations—Ideally, you already have a set of classroom expectations that have been created in collaboration with students. In addition to this, creating a set of expectations for cooperative tasks is recommended. When students engage in cooperative learning, they should know what to expect and their responsibilities as part of the group. The more they practice these, the more ingrained these expectations will be. In time, these will become a part of the learning environment and the classroom culture.
- State individual and collective goals—The cooperative learning expectations are the overarching guardrails for working together. However, for each task, the teacher should create specific goals, both for the process and the product. Some individual goals could also help increase

accountability for each student. These individual goals may be related to the roles students are assigned (discussed below).

- Assign roles—One of the most effective strategies when planning for cooperative work is clarifying roles for students. Whether you choose to assign these or give students the choice, roles can help structure the task and delineate what each student is responsible for during the time they work together. A well-known grouping strategy, POGIL, uses the following roles within small groups: manager, recorder, presenter, and reflector (Washington University in St. Louis Center, n.d.). However, you may consider creating your own roles or revising these to more clearly represent or align with the goals of the task.
- Hold each member accountable—While role assignment may help ensure that each of the students is accountable for specific goals, other ways to do this is by creating an individual as well as a collaborative assessment. As a teacher, when I used cooperative learning in the classroom, students typically had to create a group product. Whether it was a presentation or a laboratory report, the goal was that they collaborated to complete it or answer the questions. However, I also included ways to individually assess students. Sometimes, this would be in the form of a reflection at the end of the lesson or series of lessons. Other times, these would be open-ended questions about the collaborative task that were included in the unit assessment. If students were successful at answering these questions, it was evident that they engaged productively in the collaborative task and reached the learning goals.
- Be intentional about grouping decisions—Many of my former teacher candidates express their frustration about grouping students. Some allow their students to "choose" their group mates, while others are intentional about mixing things up, so to say. While I understand the rationales for both of these, I believe that teachers should have specific goals for the ways they group students. For instance, if one of the learning goals for the activity is to practice listening and understanding of diverse points of views, grouping students that have different backgrounds or interests would be important. On the other hand, if one of the goals is to encourage peer instruction, then grouping students with different abilities or performance levels (perhaps based on a previous assessment) would be ideal.

Find out the "science they know"

In addition to getting to know your students, being intentional about exposing their science pre-conceptions is vital. One of my favorite resources to use as a science teacher educator is Page Keeley's *Uncovering Student Ideas in Science*. Since its initial publication (2005), Keeley has continued to create resources for different grade levels and content areas to help teachers uncover students' scientific ideas. The resource features science probes that address scientific concepts with short scenarios or situations that are followed by one or more questions to get students engaged in reflection or discussions to decide and justify a response. Many times, these scenarios involve phenomena that students are familiar with. This allows them to use their previous knowledge to answer the question(s). In doing this, the teacher gains valuable information about science ideas that students have, as well as misconceptions that may interfere with the learning process. As you recall, this is an important part of the "Engage" stage of the 5E model. We also refer to this as pre-assessment. Therefore, probes are short scenarios that are ideal for the "Engage" part of a lesson.

Of course, the first part of the lesson is not the only time in which teachers are able to gather data about students' previous ideas. Throughout the lesson, teachers should engage in intentional observation and noticing how students are responding to and making sense of the content. Ideally, during the "explore" stage, the teacher walks around to "listen in" to students' conversations and ask questions to further students' thinking. During the next 5E stage, "explain," students' explanations are prioritized, allowing teachers to get a better picture of their understanding and an opportunity to assess it as well. The science that students know is constantly evolving. However, there are some deeply held constructs that may need revisiting. Exposing these potential misconceptions and engaging students in learning experiences that refute these is what we refer to as "conceptual change."

Be open to new ways of "doing science"

Barton discussed the idea of shifting students' (as well as teachers') constricted views of science (2003). A lot of what we see as typical "science" practices is related to laboratory work. It only takes a few seconds to conduct a quick online search using any popular search engine to see what I am referring to. However, Barton challenged teachers to think differently about what it means to "do science." In the examples she presented in her book, students engaged in design and construction of a picnic table. This was something that they wanted in the after-school program. Therefore, it was meaningful and relevant to them. While to some teachers a picnic table was not a typical product of a science project, the skills that students developed through the process were aligned to the scientific practices listed in the NGSS. For example, students had to conduct research about the different types of wood and materials needed. They had to gather data and analyze it to make decisions. They even developed a model to assess functionality of the parts. They used math when measuring the different pieces and deciding where these should be joined together. These skills were critical in going from the design to the construction of the table. Therefore, we could argue that students followed the engineering design cycle that is also part of the NGSS framework (NGSS, 2013).

NGSS's statement on diversity relates to the importance of including activities like these for students from underrepresented groups:

> From a pedagogical perspective, the focus on engineering is inclusive of students who may have traditionally been marginalized in the science classroom or experienced science as not being relevant to their lives or future. By asking questions and solving meaningful problems through engineering in local contexts (e.g., watershed planning, medical equipment, instruments for communication for the Deaf), diverse students deepen their science knowledge, come to view science as relevant to their lives and future, and engage in science in socially relevant and transformative ways. From a global perspective, engineering offers opportunities for "innovation" and "creativity" at the K-12 level. Engineering is a field that is critical to undertaking the world's challenges, and exposure to engineering activities (e.g., robotics and invention competitions) can spark interest in the study of STEM or future careers (National Science Foundation, 2010). This early engagement is particularly important for students who have traditionally not considered science as a possible career choice, including females and students from multiple languages and cultures in this global community. (NGSS Lead States, 2013, p. 438).

Maintain high expectations

When teachers focus on academic success, there are several strategies that are evident in their practice. Having high expectations is not just a mental or philosophical stance. It involves teachers identifying what "success" looks like, explicitly stating this and effectively communicating this to students. Let us consider for a moment an assignment in which students have to design and build a model of a cell. Teacher A gives students a set of instructions and criteria for evaluation. Teacher B gives students an analytic rubric that details the different areas that will be evaluated and what is considered an "Exceeds Expectations" in each of these. Teacher C gives students the same rubric and shows them exemplar models from previous years to illustrate what an excellent finished product may look like. Which of these teachers is being intentional about maintaining and communicating high expectations? I think this answer is very clear.

Through my years in academia, one feedback I have received that has helped me grow as an instructor was related to the clarity of instructions. At all grade levels, we need to be clear about what is expected of students and how they will be evaluated. Vagueness in this area may lead to discouragement, resentment, and students giving up altogether. As a result of this feedback, I have developed assignment instructions that are more detailed and specific. I accompany these with videos that go into further detail about what the expectations are. I also share examples of work from previous students (with permission, of course) to help students envision the finished product. Finally, I provide opportunities to receive feedback and revise submissions. Students should not take failure as a roadblock, but as an opportunity to improve.

Maintaining high expectations is not achieved through a single assignment or task. It is part of a culturally relevant learning environment in which teachers prioritize consistent communication about the standards and goals that are to be met. They believe that students are capable of reaching these goals as well, and this is evident in their interactions with students, the feedback they provide, and the overall classroom culture. Some other observable behaviors that I have documented of teachers that maintain high expectations are below:

- Share the standards and goals of the lessons with students at the start of the class.

- Clearly align the assignments and activities to the learning objectives and standards.
- Provide concise and specific feedback that helps students improve as needed.
- Celebrate students' accomplishments as part of structured classroom traditions.
- Provide analytic rubrics for main formative or summative assignments.
- Set and maintain clear guidelines for collaborative work, labs, and other activities.

Get feedback from students

Rarely do students have an opportunity to provide feedback to teachers about the lessons or activities they engage in. However, this is one way in which students can provide teachers with valuable information about the effectiveness of these learning experiences. Whether this effectiveness is related to their ability to comprehend the material or how well the activities engage them and connect with their realities, seeking students' feedback is an important component of critical consciousness. It is interesting that this is a common practice in higher education, but not so much in K-12. I only recall one instance in my 12 years of teaching middle and high school in which my students were asked to evaluate me as a teacher. Although this is not exactly what I am referring to, this was the only time students were asked to reflect on how effective I was as a science teacher.

The feedback I am referring to in this section is not part of a checklist within the school's improvement plan, however. To provide an example, a former pre-service teacher I supervised would give her students a ticket out the door asking them to share which of the activities from the day was more helpful towards their learning of the concepts and why. Another teacher typically included questions in her first-day survey that asked students which activities or types of assignments they preferred. These teachers understood that students' input was important when deciding on which strategies to use and assessing the effectiveness of these. When teachers gather these data and use them to evaluate their practices and make revisions, they are showing students that they have the power to make changes to their environments. This is one aspect of critical consciousness that can be implemented within your classroom space, without the need to seek to solve community problems. This is not to say that students cannot go out of the classroom and research solutions for issues that directly or indirectly affect them, of course (this is addressed in the section below). However, we cannot undermine the importance of giving students this type of agency within their immediate contexts first.

Go beyond the classroom

Embracing different ways of doing science entails going out of the classroom as well. A popular exercise in the science classroom is to ask students to draw a scientist. I have used this with my future teachers and the results are always interesting. Most individuals will draw a White man, wearing a lab coat and working with chemicals in a laboratory. The last time I tried this with my students, only one of them drew a female scientist working outdoors. Needless to say, we had a rich discussion about stereotypes in science and how teachers can help overcome these to develop their students' scientific identity.

The concept of Nature of Science (NOS) encapsulates ideas that should be understood by all students by the time they finish high school (National Science Teaching Association, 2020). These include the following:

- Scientific knowledge is simultaneously reliable and subject to change.
- Although no single universal step-by-step scientific method captures the complexity of doing science, a number of shared values and perspectives characterize a scientific approach to understanding nature.
- In general, all scientific knowledge is a combination of observations and inferences.
- Creativity is a vital, yet personal, ingredient in the production of scientific knowledge.
- Subjectivity is an unavoidable aspect of scientific knowledge.
- Science, by definition, is limited to naturalistic methods and explanations, and as such, is precluded from using supernatural elements in the production of scientific knowledge.
- A primary goal of science is the formation of theories and laws, which are terms with very specific meanings.

- Contributions to science can be made and have been made by people the world over.
- The scientific questions asked, the observations made, and the conclusions in science are to some extent influenced by the existing state of scientific knowledge, the social and cultural context of the researcher, and the observer's experiences and expectations.

In reading these statements, it becomes clear that there is not a single way of doing science or producing scientific knowledge, even when popular views may be different. The very nature of science highlights that contributions have been made by people all over the world. This includes all genders, races, ages, etc. In the same way, these contributions have been influenced by the context in which the research was conducted.

Going beyond the classroom is not limited to the physical context. The capabilities of online learning have expanded so much in the last few decades. When we go beyond the classroom context, we are opening the doors to global ways of doing science. I have seen examples of teachers that engage their students in collaboration with schools or scientific organizations from different states or countries. When we consider that by allowing students to collaborate within the classroom you are giving them an opportunity to be exposed and share divergent ideas, how much more will the richness of this interaction be with students, teachers, and scientists from around the world!

As science teachers, we need to break away from the classroom walls. The world is your classroom! During the COVID pandemic, when most of the teaching happened online, many teachers had to get creative and design lessons that engaged students in hands-on experiences at home. Students used household materials and objects to explore scientific concepts, gather data, and complete assignments. There was no need for a classroom then, there is not a need now. As a science teacher, I often used the outdoors as my classroom. My students engaged in scavenger hunts about biotic versus abiotic factors, role-plays of predator and prey interactions, sports activities to demonstrate the laws of motion, and more. During these times, the engagement in students was always higher compared to when we were learning inside the classroom. This benefit, along with the development of positive environmental attitudes, has also been explored through research in this area (Rios & Brewer, 2014).

References

Barton, A. C. (2003). *Teaching science for social justice.* Teachers College Press.

Gay, G. (2018). *Culturally responsive teaching: Theory, research, and practice.* Teachers College Press.

Hammond, Z. (2014). *Culturally responsive teaching and the brain: Promoting authentic engagement and rigor among culturally and linguistically diverse students.* Corwin Press.

Keeley, P. (2005). *Uncovering student ideas in science: Another 25 formative assessment probes.* NSTA press.

Ladson-Billings, G. (1995). But that's just good teaching! The case for culturally relevant pedagogy. *Theory Into Practice, 34*(3), 159-165.

National Science Foundation. (2010). *Preparing the next generation of STEM innovators: Identifying and developing our nation's human capital.* https://www.nsf.gov/nsb/publications/2010/nsb1033.pdf

National Science Teaching Association (NSTA). (2020, January). *Position statement-Nature of science.* https://www.nsta.org/nstas-official-positions/nature-science

NGSS Lead States. (2013). *Next Generation Science Standards: For states, by states.* The National Academies Press.

Rios, J. M., & Brewer, J. (2014). Outdoor education and science achievement. *Applied Environmental Education & Communication, 13*(4), 234–240.

Washington University in St. Louis Center for Teaching and Learning. (n.d.). *Using roles in group work.* https://ctl.wustl.edu/resources/using-roles-in-group-work/

EIGHT

Designing Culturally Relevant Science Lessons

My intention for this section was to create a template for you to use when preparing to design lessons. However, I thought it would be more useful to provide some suggestions for getting started and for how to structure the lesson. I would like to stress that even though I have used the 5E learning cycle and the NGSS framework, these decisions were based on how I picture an effective science lesson that promotes academic success. Nevertheless, before you design your lesson plan, I recommend that you identify the NGSS, state, or district standards that align with the topic that you will be teaching. Pay close attention to the observable and measurable skills listed at the beginning of each standard. This will guide how you write your objectives and assess your students. Your objectives will be simpler than the standard but will describe specifically how students will demonstrate their learning during the lesson.

After identifying the standards and important skills, consider one or two strategies you will use to assess students and ensure that they have reached your learning objectives. This is a principle of Backward Design that we currently use in our teacher education program (Wiggins & McTighe, 2005). By selecting how you will evaluate students beforehand, you will gain clarity in terms of which learning experiences have the greatest potential to help them demonstrate their learning through these. For example, if students are required to design or utilize a model of natural selection, you may assess them using a concept map or graphic organizer. Having students engage in a collaborative task with hands-on materials to demonstrate the process using the model may be a good instructional strategy to choose.

Once you have identified your objectives and assessment strategies, shift your focus to the topic or content to be covered (as stated by the standards). CRP is a lens through which you reframe your lessons, not something you "sprinkle on" after creating these or during the lesson itself. Therefore, designing a culturally relevant lesson starts with your intentionality as a teacher.

When you choose to prioritize students' cultural experiences, you give them opportunities to share their unique scientific capital and enrich the learning for all.

While reflecting on the topic, concept, and skills required, think about the students you teach. Ideally, you have gathered data at the start of the year about their background, interests, skills, and other aspects of their everyday lives and cultural wealth (see Chapter 7 for strategies to get to know your students). In other words, ideally you know more about your students than their names or other information that could be easily retrieved from a school record. Perhaps you have found out about their hobbies, interests, skills, or extracurricular activities. They may have shared with you information about their religious beliefs, their communities, or volunteer jobs. Now, is there a connection or link that could be made between your students' culture and lived experiences to the concepts that will be taught? Even if the connection is not clear or linked to the content, are there ways in which you could capitalize on some of your students' knowledge and skills when grouping them or in selecting how they will demonstrate their understanding of the content? I like to think of it this way: What are your students' expertise? What are they great at? Alternatively, you may even consider using the last part of the previous lesson (closing) to find out students' ideas related to the topic you will be teaching the next day. Of course, this may mean that you will need additional time to plan, which is not always available. However, this could give you more specific data about your students' ideas related to the new topic.

Consider ways in which you will set the stage and ensure that you are communicating high expectations from the start of the lesson. You may, for example, share the standards and objectives for the lesson and ask students to interpret these or identify terms or ideas that they are familiar with. While you may choose to use a different instructional model, I recommend you start the lesson with an engaging opening activity. Use this time to give students an opportunity to share their ideas related to the topic to be introduced. A short video about a phenomenon, an open-ended question that presents a socio-scientific issue, or a demonstration that requires students to make a prediction/hypothesis are all great opening strategies.

If the opening or "engage" has been effective, your next step is to move towards a work-session. Again, even if you do not choose to use the 5E model, I recommend that you give students an opportunity to "explore" the topic further, whether through a laboratory or stations activity, a research task, or a collaborative strategy. This could be followed by students sharing the new knowledge acquired and you expounding on it through a more formal lecture or an open discussion. As students work together to explore/explain their ideas, be intentional about asking questions that draw on their funds of knowledge. During presentations, you may ask: "How do your past experiences or background inform your understanding about this concept?" Any formative assessment strategy may be administered after this part as well. Finally, reflect on the ways that students have demonstrated learning. Consider providing multiple opportunities to do this, as well as different modes of evaluation.

While incorporating critical consciousness is a more challenging task, you may consider researching beforehand contemporary socio-scientific issues related to the topic and assigning these for homework accompanied by a reflection or writing piece. Alternatively, and probably even more effective, is to ask students to discuss their thoughts during the next day's opening activity. This creates a clear connection between the previous and current lesson. You may consider bringing additional resources or materials for students to explore in class the next day as well. Using socio-scientific issues also helps students develop scientific literacy, as they have the opportunity to practice problem-solving and decision-making. They are encouraged to reflect on their role as global citizens and on how their actions have an impact on their communities and the world as a whole.

Since you may choose to use a template, Table 8.1 below may be helpful as you prepare to design your lessons.

Lesson Plan 8.1 Culturally Relevant Lesson Plan Template

Table 8.1 Lesson template

Lesson Title:	**Grade Level:**
NGSS, State, or District Standards:	
Learning Objectives:	

NGSS 3D Areas (if applicable): Crosscutting Concepts: Science and Engineering Practices: Disciplinary Core Ideas:
Lesson Plan
Engage or Opening:
Explore or Work Session:
Explain or Lecture/Discussion:
Elaborate (if applicable):
Evaluation or Assessment Practices:
Culturally Relevant Practices
Academic Success:
Cultural Competence (include how you are incorporating students' funds of knowledge in this section as well):
Critical Consciousness:
Notes:

As you prepare to design lessons with students' cultures in mind, it is very important that we avoid making assumptions about what students' background or experiences may be based on their appearance, names, or where they are from. Instead, as you continue to get to know your students and build relationships with them, plan ways to use what you learn to create learning experiences that not only draw from their funds of knowledge but challenge them to reflect on their role as emerging scientists in their communities. Zaretta Hammond's book, *Culturally Responsive Teaching and the Brain* is one of my favorites in this area (2014). It is a main resource in my Learner Differences course. There is a powerful illustration that represents the many layers of culture as a tree (as opposed to the common iceberg representation). Hammond states: "A tree is a part of a bigger ecosystem that shapes and impacts its growth and development" (p. 24). She goes on to describe the three parts of the tree as surface (i.e., leaves), shallow (i.e., trunk), and deep (i.e., roots). If teachers truly want to embody culturally relevant teaching, culture integration needs to go beyond the surface. In other words, while noteworthy, we need to move past activities that incorporate students' language, holidays, or foods. The learning environment should acknowledge students' needs related to personal space and nonverbal modes of communication (i.e., shallow culture), for instance, as these can have a significant impact on developing trust. Most importantly, students should be engaged in experiences that allow them to share their beliefs, voice their preferences when it comes to collaborative work, and discuss their unique worldviews. These are all examples of deep culture, which Hammond notes "is what grounds the individual ... and the bedrock of self-concept, group identify, approaches to problem solving and decision making" (p. 24).

By acquiring this book, you have taken the first step toward becoming a culturally relevant science teacher. You care about your students and understand the wealth of knowledge that is in each of them, waiting to be explored. I invite you to continue learning from them and growing with them. My hope is that the lessons in this book serve as a model and inspiration for your own journey.

References

Hammond, Z. (2014). *Culturally responsive teaching and the brain: Promoting authentic engagement and rigor among culturally and linguistically diverse students.* Corwin Press.

Wiggins, G. & McTighe, J. (2005). *Understanding by design* (2nd edition). Association for Supervision and Curriculum Development.

Appendix A-Lesson Resources

Lesson 5.1-Human Activities and Biodiversity

- https://www.biofin.org/mexico#:~:text=The%20country%20is%20also%20a,medicinal%20plants%20in%20the%20country.
- https://esajournals.onlinelibrary.wiley.com/doi/full/10.1002/ecs2.1624
- https://www.worldbank.org/en/news/feature/2019/02/14/biodiversity#:~:text=Africa%20is%20home%20to%20a,as%20buffers%20to%20climate%20change.
- https://www.greenpeace.org/static/planet4-mena-stateless/2022/08/9dd732cb-biodiversity-in-the-arab-region-rajaakassab.pdf
- https://www.natureserve.org/news-releases/over-one-third-biodiversity-united-states-risk-disappearing#:~:text=They%20found%20that%20habitat%20degradation,different%20regions%20of%20the%20country

Lesson 5.2-Cultural Influences on Diet

- https://www.youtube.com/watch?v=WLbhNLbpVEQ
- https://kidshealth.org/en/kids/calorie.html
- https://www.healthychildren.org/English/healthy-living/nutrition/Pages/Energy-In-Recommended-Food-Drink-Amounts-for-Children.aspx
- https://www.myplate.gov/life-stages/kids
- https://www.verywellfit.com/recipe-nutrition-analyzer-4157076

Lesson 5.3-Exploring Mendelian Inheritance Patterns

- https://learn.genetics.utah.edu/content/basics/observable/
- https://docs.google.com/document/d/1wjmY851hxsBMWq1VXBR1poDXTGHGQ97hnjDU1TRxBts/edit
- College Board. (2021). *Pre-AP Biology Teacher Resources* (Units 3 and 4 ed.). College Board.
- Libretexts. (2022, June 9). 12.3A: Mendel's Laws of Heredity. Biology LibreTexts. https://bio.libretexts.org/Bookshelves/Introductory_and_General_Biology/Book%3A_General_Biology_(Boundless)/12%3A_Mendel's_Experiments_and_Heredity/12.03%3A_Laws_of_Inheritance/12.3A%3A_Mendels_Laws_of_Heredity

Lesson 5.4-Diversity Benefits Us All

- https://gen.uga.edu/documents/biodiversity/activities/Biomes%20who%20what%20lives.pdf
- https://www.youtube.com/watch?v=zkEbI_d6Uxw&t=40s

- https://unfoundation.org/blog/post/biodiversity-explained-facts-myths-and-the-race-to-protect-it/

Lesson 5.5-Rhymes and Rhythms of the Body

- https://www.canva.com/design/DAFvy4OJK9M/33sYqFGB8x6Z7QyzGZsl-g/edit
- https://www.youtube.com/watch?v=KSbbDnbSEyM&list=PLn0DCiMMuRy8ZJK0QbGLY7aAC1Ei5wbWN&index=1
- https://www.easyayurveda.com/2020/03/12/interrelationship-systems/
- https://docs.google.com/document/d/1ZKPJCPTEzvvb8xWD2jV4VavIGHPywDdwFhpiEFYyxZ8/edit

Lesson 5.6-How Do Fireworks Work?

- https://www.youtube.com/watch?v=2OLC51rzLSI
- https://docs.google.com/document/d/1LKWAIR0bWoWcwY8QCqaxULor5UR_6y83mQiylxTEmvU/edit
- https://www.kwintessential.co.uk/blog/culture/fireworks-world-celebrates
- https://earth.org/environmental-impact-of-fireworks/

Lesson 5.7-Energy Transformations

- https://docs.google.com/document/d/1SBBMaGOmGuITmJCNumt3PxJjgQtmDlV296rtALuQulI/edit?usp=sharing
- https://phet.colorado.edu/en/simulations/energy-skate-park

Lesson 5.8-Heat Transfer in the Kitchen

- https://youtu.be/nKjJuGRqgKA?si=XXWtjByrruiIBDZS
- https://www.webstaurantstore.com/blog/4340/types-of-heat-transfer-in-cooking.html
- https://med.libretexts.org/Courses/Kansas_State_University/FNDH_413%3A_Science_of_Food/01%3A_Food_Safety_and_Preparation/1.02%3A_Food_Preparation/1.2.05%3A_Understanding_Heat
- https://energy5.com/the-science-of-heat-transfer-in-energy-efficient-cooking

Lesson 5.9-Little Star

- https://www.kent.edu/mdj/news/professor-researches-link-between-genetics-social-media-use#:~:text=He%20found%20that%20while%20both,to%20our%20underlying%20genetic%20traits
- https://dnalc.cshl.edu/view/17001-Punnett-Square-Blank.html

Lesson 6.1-Renewable Sources of Energy Around the World

- https://ourworldindata.org/renewable-energy
- https://www.climatecouncil.org.au/11-countries-leading-the-charge-on-renewable-energy/
- https://www.iea.org/reports/global-energy-review-2021/renewables

- https://beakersandink.com/how-to-teach-claims-evidence-and-reasoning-cer-like-a-pro/

Lesson 6.2-Sport Injuries

- https://online.csp.edu/resources/infographic/common-sports-injuries/
- https://www.hopkinsmedicine.org/health/conditions-and-diseases/sports-injuries/sports-injury-statistics
- https://www.nfhs.org/articles/the-role-of-athletic-directors-in-injury-prevention/
- https://kidshealth.org/en/parents/sports-safety.html

Lesson 6.3-Exploring Friction

- https://www.thinkingmaps.com/cdn/WhitePaper-BuildingBlocksofBrainBasedLearning.pdf
- https://beakersandink.com/how-to-teach-claims-evidence-and-reasoning-cer-like-a-pro/
- https://avretaros.medium.com/speed-in-sports-79b9a0f2caed

Lesson 6.4-Genetically Modified Foods

- https://www.insider.com/guides/health/diet-nutrition/gmo-pros-and-cons#:~:text=Advantages%20of%20GMO%20foods%20include,reactions%20or%20increased%20antibiotic%20resistance
- https://www.ncbi.nlm.nih.gov/pmc/articles/PMC3791249/
- https://www.who.int/news-room/questions-and-answers/item/food-genetically-modified

About the Authors

Suzanna Roman-Oliver has been an educator for almost 20 years. She was a high school science teacher for English Language Learners for 12 years. After that, she worked as a Clinical Assistant Professor at Kennesaw State University. Her dissertation research, the inspiration for this book, focused on pre-service teachers, understanding and implementation of culturally relevant pedagogy during their student-teaching experience. Dr. Roman-Oliver continues to do research to explore the influence of culture in the teaching and learning of science. She lives in Rome, Georgia with her husband, son, and puppy. She is currently an Assistant Professor at Georgia College and State University.

About the Contributors

Sarah Brown is an aspiring middle-grade educator currently in the teacher preparation program at Georgia College and State University (GCSU). As a student in the John H. Lounsbury College of Education, she is working towards certification in both middle grades science and English. Her passion for working with English Language Learners (ELL) started early on in her education. Seeing students light up as they grasped new concepts and gained confidence in their language abilities fueled her interest in becoming a teacher. Through her coursework and field experiences at GCSU, she has gained valuable hands-on training in engaging diverse learners. Her student teaching placement in a local middle school allowed her to utilize the latest ELL teaching strategies under the guidance of a master teacher. This experience confirmed for her that fostering an inclusive classroom where students feel valued is crucial for learning. As she embarked on her first year teaching in the fall of 2023, she aims to create a supportive environment for her students to take risks and grow. Her ultimate goal is to help each student reach their full potential. She is thrilled to start this next chapter doing what she loves—teaching and empowering students.

Tara Conner grew up in South Georgia. She currently teaches high school biology and environmental science in Rochelle, Georgia. The students in Mrs. Conner's classes are mostly from rural areas. Many of them are from farm families and work on family farms. They enjoy participating in sports or outdoor activities such as hunting. Mrs. Conner is also a registered nurse and maintains her credentials. Her goal is to help bring students together, helping them realize the impact their differences and experiences can have on the world. She desires for students to experience science and learn important concepts so that they can function and thrive in this scientifically sophisticated and complex world. She enjoys seeing students achieve beyond their expectations and connect scientific concepts to real life experiences. Mrs. Conner seeks to engage her students and glean from their prior knowledge of science concepts and practices taught in earlier grades and strengthen them as her class progresses.

Larry Layfield has taught high school chemistry for 3 years and teaches in the same county he grew up in. He always loved science because of the nature of inquiry and systematic approach to answering questions. He pursued teaching to inspire and introduce students to science. As a teacher, Larry seeks to incorporate culturally responsive pedagogy and phenomenon-based learning to facilitate acquiring knowledge in chemistry. In the spring of 2023, Larry was selected as the local school teacher of the year and enjoys spending time with friends and family.

Perri Lennon is a middle school science teacher in Georgia. Her passions have always been teaching, learning, and social advocacy for world peace. In education, Perri found a job that would encompass all her passions—she could educate, she could be educated, and she could contribute to the greater good of our social economy. As an educator at an immensely diverse school, she believes it is important to be culturally inclusive. She strives to encourage the dissemination of insights into various cultural backgrounds through classwork, to create a learning environment that promotes cultural diversity, acceptance, and student success. Having experienced so many impactful and inspiring educators through her time as a student in Fulton County, she feels that she, too, can have a lasting impact on her students. Perri believes the small positive actions she is taking in her classroom are capable of having far-reaching impacts on the world, causing a ripple effect for inclusivity and peace.

Anne Norviel is a biology teacher at Aquinas High School, a Catholic school in Augusta, Georgia. She has been teaching for 8 years. She is a wife and the mother of two children. Anne is a proud graduate of Augusta University, where she fell in love with science, more specifically, the health sciences. Her career in teaching was unexpected, and she is thankful for the opportunity to share her passion for the sciences with her high school students. Recently, Anne returned to Georgia College and State University and proudly added a Masters of Art in Teaching in Secondary Science to her resume. She creates lessons that are student-centered and hands-on. Anne's approach to teaching is focused on making learning tangible in order to allow students more opportunities to better understand and connect with the material. Anne strives to create lessons that keep students engaged and excited about learning. She desires to leave a lasting impact on her students.

Barbara J. Parks is a Health Educator with two decades of experience in public health, human services, academia, and the K-12 public school system. She holds a bachelor's degree in Sports Medicine: Athletic Training from Georgia College and State University, a MS degree in Community Health from Howard University, and an M.A.T. in Health/Kinesiology from Georgia College and State University. In addition, she is nationally certified as a Certified Health Education Specialist (CHES) of 15 years. The Georgia native still resides in the state she loves and continues to educate public school scholars. She enjoys educating students on health principles, in hopes of empowering them to adopt and maintain healthy behavior practices that last throughout their lifespan. When she is not teaching, Barbara spends most of her time reading, exercising, watching poetry slams and writing poetry, and catching her favorite sports shows. *The Science I Know—Culturally Relevant Science Lessons from Secondary Classroom* is her first book as a contributing author.

Ansley Talafous is a dedicated and aspiring educator currently in her senior year at Georgia College and State University, where she is pursuing a bachelor's degree in Middle Grades Education with a concentration in Science and

Language Arts. As part of her academic journey, Ansley is presently engaged in her senior internship in a 7th-grade science classroom, where she collaborates with approximately 100 general education and PEC students to teach life science. Her teaching philosophy seamlessly integrates theoretical knowledge with hands-on experience, a fusion cultivated through 2 consecutive years of student teaching across various grade levels. Beyond the classroom, Ansley actively participates in extracurricular activities on her college campus and seizes professional development opportunities to continually enhance her educational skills. Fueled by a deep sense of responsibility and dedication to the field of education, Ansley eagerly looks forward to making a significant contribution to shaping the minds of future generations. Her holistic approach to education reflects a commitment to nurturing well-rounded individuals through both academic and extracurricular pursuits.

Melissa Volante is a high school physical and environmental science teacher at a school located south of Atlanta, Georgia. She is in her 7th year of teaching and recently earned her master's degree in secondary education from Georgia College and State University. In addition to teaching, she is leading the Fellowship of Christian Athletes school huddle, leading her high-school academic focus class in developing a PBIS program for the middle school, working as one of the facilitators for Chick-Fil-A Leader Academy, and serving as part of the Summer Bridge Program team which seeks to prepare and equip incoming freshmen to succeed in high school. She is passionate about helping her students develop and succeed in academics as well as all other areas of life and believes strongly in getting to know each child individually in order to educate most effectively. Although she loves teaching, Melissa's favorite and most important roles are wife, mom of three, and follower of Jesus. Melissa loves music, exercise, spending time with friends and family, trying new restaurants, and visiting new places.

Roman-Oliver Index

The Science I Know

Name and Subject Index

Roman-Oliver Index

The Science I Know

Lesson Plan Index